The Wake Forest Series of Irish Poetry VOLUME 1

The Wake Forest Series of

Irish Poetry

VOLUME ONE

Harry Clifton
Dennis O'Driscoll
David Wheatley
Sinéad Morrissey
& Caitríona O'Reilly

Selected and with a Preface
by Jefferson Holdridge

Wake Forest University Press

Designed by Richard Eckersley. Text set in Trinité
Printed in the United States of America
Library of Congress Control Number: 2004117690

ISBN 1-930630-20-4

Contents

Preface

The Wake Forest Series of Irish Poetry: Volume 1 is a representative anthology meant to introduce to a broader audience a number of Irish poets, some young, some in their prime, who have not appeared widely before in North America. The poets of this inaugural volume are Harry Clifton, Dennis O'Driscoll, David Wheatley, Sinéad Morrissey, and Caitríona O'Reilly. From the burgeoning economic realities of the "Celtic Tiger" to the burden of religious and political realignment, from urban scenes to historical landscapes, these poets sensitively record the effects of writing in a society that has shifted dramatically in the last decades; however, they do not write solely from historical or social contexts, but also out of psychological compulsions or in a mythic mode. Whatever their subject, they write with an awareness of the formal traditions and tensions of Irish poetry.

HARRY CLIFTON

Born in Dublin (1952), and educated in English literature and philosophy in Ireland, Harry Clifton has spent many years living and working abroad.[1] The combination of literary/philosophical interests and long-time travel abroad has provided much of the intellectual and emotional impetus behind his poetry. From the very first poem in this selection, "The Waking Hour," Clifton is concerned with perception, sexuality, the sacred and profane, the prerogatives and ethics of power, and, most importantly, the ability of the imagination to help us persevere. Love and the sexual act constitute the best challenge to human failings, wherein we deliver "To our disembodied selves / Wherever we are, the temporal fruits / Of Eden, the past and future again." This conjunction between sexuality, with its roots in our animal nature, and higher forms of love may account for his long interest in St. Augustine, one of the early fathers of Christianity, famous among other reasons for his understanding of the relationship between the sacred and profane. From the early poem "The Walls of Carthage" to his very recent poem "Reading Saint Augustine," Clifton appears as one condemned to shuttle endlessly back and forth across the desert between Alexandria (the center of the empire) and Carthage

1. See appendix for biographical information on each poet.

(the periphery), seemingly confined to the desert of relativity. As Clifton has himself stated:

> Out of that image [of endless shuttling] I wrote "The Walls of Carthage," one of the earliest poems in this selection [*The Desert Route*], and one which, in a sense, defines all the journeys of *The Desert Route* — for the polarities called Alexandria and Carthage might just as easily be North and South, id and consciousness, the West and elsewhere. And the desert between them, physical and fleshed out though I hope it is in these poems, [is] no more than a state of mind.

Clifton's "state of mind" is more an artistic than religious epiphany or revelation. Art might provide the reconciliation between the ethical demands of the spirit and consciousness and the sensual demands of the body and id. Clifton's fascination with the religious theme and the sinful life of the saint has not changed over the years, nor has his feeling that what Augustine could not reconcile in his life and times, through the antagonism between the spirit and flesh, he cannot reconcile in his: "For all its cloud-apocalypse funeral pyres / Women, it seemed, would have the final word." The poem "Søren Kierkegaard" makes similar claims for the sensual life as the basis of the successful philosophical life. Clifton's domain is large and his ambition to write impersonal, challenging poetry life-long.

The argument between body and mind, in all its manifestations, remains a constant theme throughout Clifton's work, from "Death of Thomas Merton" to the poems of *God in France*. In the former poem, Clifton sees the death of Thomas Merton as indicative of a philosophical quandary at the heart of the Vietnam era. Merton was a Trappist monk who accidentally died of electrocution in Bangkok in 1968, at the height of the Vietnam War, on a mission to explore links between Christianity and Buddhism. The scene for Clifton becomes one of crucifixion. The Vietnam era is among the most potent demonstrations of the Enlightenment predicament, where a technologically superior army (playing the part of Reason in Clifton's polarities) cannot control a hidden enemy in a guerilla campaign, because of its ability to live in a network of tunnels, appearing and disappearing like a subconscious force. Clifton's historical perspective is that we live in "an age of anxiety" threatened by the revolt of the irrational, of which the Vietnam War was exemplary. In this, he is heir to Auden's generation, particularly to the Irish poet Louis MacNeice, whom he greatly admires. Aware of his role as poet within an increasingly skeptical age, Clifton meditates in the *Metre* pamphlet *God in France* on the idea of God existing in what he views as an unbelieving country. Even Clifton's taste in art reflects such concerns. In "Euclid Avenue" the personal world is described as dispersed among the conflicting energies that make up modern and postmodern life. The only future for the individual is to "disappear again / In a private wilderness." To Clifton, the subjective life is more meaningful when perceived as part of something larger; hence his taste for the impersonal in poetry. The web of personal feelings and sensations that supposedly make us more individual tend, in fact, to mark our collectivization and conformity. He sees significant correspondence between the energies released individually and the movements of history. The later poem "The Poet Sandro Penna, in Old Age" tells a story of isolation, but with more pointed social significance; for Sandro Penna was an Italian poet, anathematized in some literary circles for his sexual proclivities, who died in Rome in 1976. The figure of the artist, marginalized by the philosophical, religious and political poverty of his age, is also explored in "Absinthe in New Orleans." In truth, this figure is the hallmark of all his work.

Clifton's earliest poems are taken from *The Liberal Cage* (1988) and from *The Desert Route* (1992). The latter is an anthology of poems collected from *The Liberal Cage* and *The Walls of Carthage* (1977), which is introduced by Derek Mahon for The Gallery Press. The themes of early poems (along with religion, sexuality and philosophy) include colonization, life in Africa ("Latitude 5°N"), Asia ("Monsoon Girl") and America ("Euclid Avenue," "Absinthe at New Orleans"), and the Vietnam War ("Death of Thomas Merton"). Like many of his generation, born in the Fifties, Clifton left Ireland because there was little work to be had there. For Clifton, it was a life lived elsewhere in a state of "unbelonging," as he has termed it, self-consciously acquired in many places along the way. The title poem of his volume of selected poems, "The Desert Route," provides the landscape for such feeling, and the ellipses in the poem are illustrative of the disrupted consciousness of unbelonging. The only operative force in the poem is trade: the local, ancient trade routes that run through the desert and the global routes over land and sea. Globalization has diminished the power of the individual, as mirrored in the idiot at the center of this poem. Political and economic forces have become the force of destiny, in which the individual is a colonized subject. The only hope for freedom is the movement of the gentle goat — the prodding of the sexual life, the last precinct of the self, which even aggressive commodification cannot quite control, and which transgresses national boundaries.

Deracination is another compellingly explored theme in Clifton's poetry of transgressed boundaries. Throughout his philosophical and religious enquiries, time and place are indelibly marked as states exiled from truth and grace, in which the estranged speaker can only meditate on causes that are out of his control. To paraphrase Maeve Brennan, Clifton is a poet in exile who knows of a country that makes all other countries seem strange. Yet his exile is ending. He and his wife, the novelist Deirdre Madden, have returned to Ireland after many years of living abroad. His reaction to the transformed country should be illuminating. Cultural pluralism will define the future in Ireland. A certain type of deracination has already begun through the thousands of refugees and immigrants who have entered the country in the last decade. It is fitting, then, that the early poems also record the first part of his journey through Africa and Asia. Colonization, or the experience of the postcolonial, has been a controversial talking point for some time in Ireland. In Clifton, these themes are chiefly concerned with the life of people of color, those very people who now make up part of the Irish population. "Monsoon Girl" was controversial when it was written, and might be again were it set now among the foreign dancers in the nightclubs of Dublin. The parallels between the social system as it functioned within the colonies and the society created by the escape to the center (in this case Europe) after the colonial collapse are compelling. Ireland's middle position between colonized at home and beneficiary of the color line abroad makes it a complex figure of the various competing social dynamics of the postcolonial world. In this poem, sexuality delineates (among other issues) the limits and possessions of power in Ireland and elsewhere.

The poems from *Night Train through the Brenner* (1994) reflect Clifton's time in Europe and, interestingly enough, say a great deal about Ireland's past rather than its future, particularly those poems which concern village life. Clifton has lived in Paris for the last ten years with a one-year stay in the mountains of the Abruzzi, in central Italy, a time he described in the prose memoir *On the Spine of Italy* (1999). Compared to one of the metropolitan centers of postmodern life, the Abruzzi must have presented a strong contrast. His thoughts on his time there are best represented by the figure of Ignazio Silone, chronicler of village life in the mountains of the Abruzzi in central Italy during the 1930s. The Italian's books, *Fontamara* and *Bread and Wine*, are studies in the failure of the poor to unite against the forces of church and state. Exiled in Switzerland from 1930 to 1945 for his fascist politics, Silone died in 1978 and is buried in the Abruzzi. Clifton concludes his poem "At the Grave of Silone" with an epitaph to these "Disheartened villages," in which "Memory tries to wake / Blind monuments to the Fascist dead," as well as to "men who cannot shake / The ant of toil from their Sunday clothes." For Silone, like some other modern Italian thinkers, the answer to social injustice was found in reconciling the most potent symbols of Italian thought: "The Christian cross, the Communist rose." Such reconciliation is the aim of many Italian thinkers in the twentieth century. What makes Silone especially important to Clifton the poet is his value for the "human word." In many of Clifton's poems from *Night Train through the Brenner* the human word wakes memory from its torpor and sometimes softens the hardship. A resolution to find meaning in human activity, whether familial or social, pervades the descriptions of the harsh landscape around the Gran Sasso. There is a sense that, in living "In Earthquake Country," the human word is forced to root "itself in the inhuman."

It is a quality Clifton would like to emulate, and which he feels is akin to the stoic philosophy of the Irish in a similarly merciless countryside. The Abruzzi region, lying on the spine of Italy, is often compared to the Mezzogiorno in Southern Italy, which is usually defined as everything south of Rome. The inhabitants of the remote areas in both regions exhibit a singularly premodern sensibility. The various poems, "Watershed," "In Hoc Signo," "Taking the Waters," "The Better Portion," all attempt to assess the aesthetic of landscape which Clifton traces along the backbone of the Apennines. The poems give little expectation of renewal and transcendence that isn't bitterly felt or even resented by anyone with experience of the outside world. The poetic conceit itself is seen as a form of betrayal, as the closing images from "Crossing the Apennines" illustrate. While walking through "impossibly high meadows" of the high plateaus that distinguish this remote and savage region (where wolves still roam), Clifton comes upon a herd of "silent horses" who surround him "like trusting spirits / Expecting sugar"; it is an image of trust which the poet, like the land, quickly undercuts: "and we fed them salt." This feeling of having been given a gift from his time spent living among the inhabitants of the Abruzzi, and having little to give in return, suffuses all these poems, and in "The Canto of Ulysses" — a celebration of the physical life — this feeling is most clearly articulated. The poem is based on the lines from Dante's *Inferno*, Canto 26, in which Ulysses and his companions sail west of the known world (Gibraltar) and perish by shipwreck within sight of the earthly paradise. It is significant that this Canto renewed Primo Levi's sense of his own humanity during the dehumanization of the concentration camps. Such an experience forms the crucible for postmodern consciousness, and is one which Clifton consistently outlines in his poetry. Like Dante's Ulysses, he seemingly can never return home and therefore must find sustenance in his journey. The last lines are like a letter to the people he leaves behind on this island of time.

In Clifton's more recent poems, the predicament has sometimes presented itself in personal or artistic terms. In "Bare Arm," from the *Metre* publication *God in France*, two people catch each other undressed in opposing windows, lit by "stray lightings." Experiencing this, they are "Alive in the forest / Of second nature." The important pun on second nature presents a small revelatory chance that, though our first nature has at least been partially eclipsed, there is some chance of seeing instinctually again. Instinctual knowledge may survive the various philosophical, religious, and political assaults of contemporary existence. Art, or poetry, of course, reveals its own forest of forms in which second natures may be revealed, as is evident in "Reductio." Art presents the best chance for the reconciliation of the intellectual and ethical claims existence makes on us, almost at times to life-denying degrees, because it allows scope for the irrational needs of our nature, and, more importantly, gives shape to them while we are trapped in the desert of relative values ("Saharas spread") until, with

> A glass suspended in air —
> You take a drink. To keep your fingers warm
> You busy yourself, with the one loved face
> Attempted endlessly, with the one loved form.

DENNIS O'DRISCOLL

Dennis O'Driscoll's poetry revolves around the world of business and the working day. One could say that the civil servant O'Driscoll, born in 1954, includes everything in his poetry that the lawyer Wallace Stevens excludes from his: the competitiveness of the office, the various lusts and callousness of the workaday world, the inevitable sense of being "over the hill" and of having failed if only because the terms of success are so elusive. His poetry has followed the frustrations and fulfillments of living in the suburbs of Dublin and working in the civil service through the seventies, eighties and nineties. These are the stuff of O'Driscoll's poetic and he wields them to fine effect. Nevertheless, it is not merely subject that proves the depth of his poetic powers; it is his ability to write skillfully in various poetic styles.

The earliest poem in this selection, "Someone" (from the volume *Kist*), 1982, captures the droll but compassionate nature of his quotidian poetic. It also displays his ability to give a sardonic twist to a cliché at its end: "someone today is seeing the world for the last time / as innocently as he had seen it first." In "Stillborn," "Conception," and "Spoiled Child" (from *Hidden Extras*, 1987), O'Driscoll sensitively uses comparable techniques to connect stillbirth and its effects on parents to civilization's struggles with its own conception, and its own stillbirth. The cumulative irony of the list of long lines in "Someone" gives way in the other poems to precision and lyric voice. In his revision of the 1987 version of "Stillborn," O'Driscoll concludes of parents' grief: "What we are lamenting / Is our flesh and blood, this child / That has not laughed or cried / This mild May morning." In "Spoiled Child" O'Driscoll is philosophical: "my child will not be a comfort to my old age / my child will not be cheated or promoted or denied . . . its blemishes, its beauty, its shortcomings and promise." The unborn child platonically remains "forever unsullied and unfulfilled." In "Conception," this careful meditation becomes a biblical and historical figure: "scum of humanity / seed of pain . . . a lost civilisation / bedclothes stain."

The poems selected from the volume *Long Story Short* (1993), particularly "Fruit Salad" and "Misunderstanding & Musak," exhibit another side of O'Driscoll. The latter poem is central to O'Driscoll's *oeuvre*; a wry description of two people in two different shopping markets, buying food for the meal they are meant to share, who are threatened by the catastrophe which hovers near them in the random violence of this mechanized world: "It is 6:55. You may have been murdered. / It is 6:55. I may have been flattened by a truck." In "Fruit Salad" there is a celebration of the sensual life, the *quidditas*, the whatness of the world of fruit. Peach, strawberry, pear and apple, each has its own character, its own traditional place in the perspectives of human consciousness. The peach seems to contain all fruits within its "palette; / colours dart from apricot to apple," while the strawberry is "a precious stone / cut one and expose the marbled core." The pear "hangs in a shaft of autumn light / timeless as a bronze cathedral bell" and the apple leads us "back to that first temptation," inviting us to bite "the way back to a primal silence." The object world thankfully provides an iconography of the various states of being with which to soothe the loss and pain of the preceding poems. "Residuary Estates" and "Reading Primo Levi on a Train," also from *Long Story Short*, remind us of the constant need for this iconography, that the very poems which describe suffering are palliatives themselves. Poetry may not offer the consolations of philosophy, but it can supply an aesthetic form through which the inconsolable nature of suffering (in this case the death of the poet"s mother) may be viewed philosophically. In this way, O'Driscoll finds a deeply humanist, but demanding perspective on his subject. In "Residuary Estates," his mother lies "wasted by illness / left for dead / flowers rooted / in her soiled body." The poet reflects: "to weigh so little / she must have taken / enormous pains." Like many of his mordant puns, the pun at the end of the poem is too painful to be cynical. O'Driscoll feels that it is impossible to enjoy life without being aware of, and haunted by, the larger doom that awaits so much of humanity, as the poem dedicated to the writing of the concentration camp survivor, Primo Levi, makes clear. It has a direct bearing on the celebration that is "Fruit Salad." Reading Levi transforms the image of the ordinary: "A woman cradles a package — slop bucket or lampshade?" The suggestion that every lampshade might be made of human skin is one that must indict the enactment of our daily routines, "the ordered peace / of our atrocity-free mornings."

In the poems from his most recent volumes, *Quality Time* (1997), *Weather Permitting* (1999) and *Exemplary Damages* (2002), which form the largest part of this selection, O'Driscoll has found his subject most fully. The tensions in his own life between his career in the civil service and his life as a poet are mirrored in the larger relationship within Ireland between economic success and the traditional folklife that has undergone such radical change. "Them and You" is a poem about selfhood and community, in which the reader is assumed to be part of the new Ireland and "them" the representatives of the old: "They look weathered. / You look tanned." Or, more pointedly, "They knock back pints. / You cultivate a taste for vintage wines." Though the poem predates the Celtic Tiger, it outlines the parameters of what has since occurred in Ireland, as the poet tries to weigh the sense of what is being lost and gained in an economically and culturally transitional period. In the end, however, the poems from these volumes convince one of O'Driscoll's poetic powers because he is able to work within a variety of poetic models.

In the poem entitled "Water," for instance, he ably shifts poetic register to broaden the scope of his ordinary subject. He begins the poem with his notable comic flair. Water is a "miracle" because it does not taste of "peat," "chlorine," "old tap fittings" or "dead sheep." He moves from an aesthetic meditation, "Water was the first mirror, / drinking images of beauty," to a political and scientific one, "Water clings to its neutrality, / changes state at boiling point," and then on to a sensual one in which water "finds the level at which / tensions cool, limbs relax." Finally he closes with a religious parallel, synthesizing the rest: "It is . . . the burst main flooding / from Christ's frozen side." The ability to shift register gives credence to those critical truisms on the characteristics of contemporary Irish poetry: O'Driscoll has a "Dutch painter's eye for detail," a "gift for the ordinary," an "ability to transform the everyday world into the extraordinary." The sequence *The Bottom Line* (first published separately by Dedalus Press in 1994) combines the poet's numerous strengths and, although a pessimistic portrayal of middle management existence, gives a strong sense of stoic perseverance and a real, if distant, hope for redemption. This sequence is his most probing, personal treatment of this subject matter. Here the stakes are made clear. O'Driscoll has said that the poem arose out of a moment in which he was "shocked to see himself looking like a bureaucrat taking out his credit card." The voices are those of various businessmen and bureaucrats poised at differing levels of the hierarchical scale. It begins with various images of corporate cruelty and greed, moves through reflections on the speakers' careers and personal life, and ends with his facing the dubious sum of his ambition. The poem contains many sharp insights into corporate and contemporary Western life, and often reads like a poetic version of Joseph Heller's novel *Something Happened*. It also contains some exact imagery, as, for example, when the poet notes the "sheer / vertiginous layers of stacked light" in a modern office building. Perhaps the most palpable feeling is of failure: "Then the time comes when you know / none of your promise will be fulfilled." We must accept "failure in good / heart, battling home against the wind / this night the same as the last." The poet has said of this stanza, "That's depressing, but once I wrote it I knew it was the truest stanza for me that I've ever written." It is this unflinching eye that gives his poetry its strength.

The poems of *Weather Permitting* rehearse some old themes with adroitness and sympathy. Here O'Driscoll begins to remember friends lost either through death or long absence ("Either"). "Nor" takes up the ironic stance of "Someone," listing all the forms of unnecessary suffering which await us: "There didn't have to be 2,000 diseases / of the skin." I remember someone commenting. / Nor 17,293 painfully slow routes through the vomitory / Before being thrown to the lions of death." It ends with a twist concerning the unnecessary newborns "added / to the tally, since the opening line." "In Memory of Alois Alzheimer" plays on the irony that Alzheimer's name is remembered each time someone begins to lose one's memory, while "Tomorrow" posits that the future promises happiness because of the blank sheet of its anonymity. The title poem, "Weather Permitting," accomplishes a beautiful summarization of O'Driscoll's themes, exploring the question, "Balm of mind and body. Will we ever feel / more reconciled to life than now?"

In his most recent volume, *Exemplary Damages,* the effects are felt in terms of growing old, both individually and collectively. In O'Driscoll's rendering, Irish society is being tried and tested by the changes it has unconsciously or consciously embraced, changes which have sometimes made it almost unrecognizable to the Irish themselves. Where once the conditions were religious or familial, now they are economic, and the damages are "exemplary" for mainly humorous reasons. The implicit criticism is that these examples are insufficient to their purported moral ends. Similarly, the poet contends that economics cannot provide society and individual with answers in the face of decay and death. In "Missing God," Ireland's lost faith is lamented for the diminishment of poetic power and personal strength that attends the loss ("and our contracted hearts lose a beat"). This question becomes an artistic as well as social question: Does the quotidian world become a quagmire if we reduce our world view to the importance of the empirical, the everyday? The question is germane to the aesthetic of the entire volume and indeed to O'Driscoll's entire career.

The strengths of *Exemplary Damages* are familiar to readers of O'Driscoll's work. The poems are full of careful observations of political and social life in Ireland. The poet has come to be known by his subject matter and his compassionate voice. In "Thrush and Anti-Thrush," the struggle between the poet's love of inspiration versus the poet's necessary regard for truth (here, as in many recent Irish poems, aligned with the realist aesthetic of the Dutch) is insightfully played out for the reader. The "Dutch toss / pickled herrings down the hatch. // Enough rubbish you'd assume to choke the drains of any gullet," he writes, but then notes that even in the most realistic art, if it is of the highest quality, "you catch / the rapturous return journey of song." The poet captures the struggle with rhetorical finesse. Poetry must record the rubbish as it accumulates, but must continue to listen to the "rococo notes that cry out for transcribing / on calf parchment with a calligraphy quill." Within these later volumes, there are various references to bird flight, which is behind that "journey of song" and which stands for the act of writing poetry. It is a movement which claims some of the strongest or most poetic writing in the book, as in "Full Flight." The poem of an "overhead jet" beautifully balances the imperatives of fact (in this case, mechanical flight) and the imagination.

It might equally be
a speeded-up version

of Bede's fable:
a mechanical sparrow

hightailing it above
that transient banquet hall.

It also explores themes of modernity and religion while skillfully implying that the present end of Christianity continues to seek religious metaphors amidst the ephemera of experience, much as did the age of Bede at the rise of the Christian faith: on the wings of a bird or a plane, on the flight of the imagination, at the edge of transcendence. When O'Driscoll keeps to the poetry of the object world and balances the rhetoric of the mundane with imaginative fire, avoiding reportage, allowing the poem to achieve sustained metaphorical insight, he leads us "from the desert of downtown," as he writes in "So Much Depends" (indebted to William Carlos Williams), back "to the promised land of the red barn." This poem uses a great deal of religious imagery (vows, the Amish, cathedrals, sheep and goats, wheat and chaff, even Grandma Moses) to develop its sense of the red barn as an iconic place exerting an almost numinous hold on the urban imagination: a symbol of plenty and bounty, of things saved, of immortal corn. The last poem in the selection reminds us that achieving metaphorical insight is a "Vigil" that "You are the only reliable witness to when / the light is separated from the darkness."

DAVID WHEATLEY

When David Wheatley was a student at Trinity he edited the student magazines *Icarus* and *College Green*, an apprenticeship which has served him in good stead, for he is one of the founding editors of *Metre*, a poetry journal coming out of Ireland, England and the Czech Republic that is noted for its perspicacious, often controversial reviews and articles. In this journal, Wheatley, along with Justin Quinn and Caitríona O'Reilly among others, has certainly questioned the rules of poetry reviewing in Ireland, particularly the reviewing of poets on poets, which Dennis O'Driscoll has characterized as "insider trading," even if they have been accused of assuming a few inside rules (and reviews) of their own. Wheatley, like Sinéad Morrissey and O'Reilly, and much of his generation, and unlike the generation of Clifton and O'Driscoll, has an advanced graduate degree. Born in 1970, Wheatley wrote his Ph.D. on the poetry of Beckett, a writer who has remained a primary interest and influence for him. The trend of obtaining advanced degrees is a product of a growing economy that for the first time has the ability to offer fellowships and scholarships and that promises some prospect for future careers. What effect this change will have on Irish poetry remains to be seen, but it is inevitable and has saved at least part of a generation from enforced exile. For Wheatley, it has allowed him to be a poet-critic. He brings a critical presence to bear on his poetry, reflected in his choice of subject matter, which covers such topics as bedsits (rather cramped studio apartments, usually home to students or the poor) and sleepwalking, and such settings as China, Eastern Europe, and France. He writes poetry that combines a formal discipline with an intellectual range, and which can claim subjects as diverse as Homer Simpson and the 19th-century Irish poet James Clarence Mangan. His poetry is panoptic at times, and personal at others, sometimes ventriloquist or virtuoso.

The title of David Wheatley's first volume *Thirst*, published by Gallery Press in 1997, is taken from Beckett's line, "thirsting away, you don't know what for." His second book is entitled *Misery Hill* (published by Gallery in 2000), and a poetry-pamphlet, co-written with Caitríona O'Reilly and entitled *Three-Legged Dog*, was published by Wild Honey Press in 2003. In his first volume, *Thirst*, there are poems of tender personal insight ("Visiting Hour" and "Sleepwalking"), on the intricacies of human relationships ("Table Manners"), on the historical and cultural emblems of the Dublin cityscape ("Autumn, the Nightwalk, the City, the River") and others of artistic homage ("Giacometti, c. 1952" and "Spleen"). Many of these subjects are evident in this second volume, *Misery Hill* and in those of his forthcoming volume *Terrestrial Variations.* There are nevertheless exceptions in his first volume ("AM Radio," "A Garden in September," and "At a Yüan Play") that indicate another aspect of his later development. In each of these three poems, there is a balance between personal investment in the subject and his intellectual curiosity and engagement. This balance is a harbinger of what is most successful in poems from *Misery Hill* and *Terrestrial Variations.* Wheatley's poetry is particularly effective when assessing his own experience or when projecting himself impersonally onto his subject, as in the "Sonnets to James Clarence Mangan," which contains some of the most important poems from the first two volumes. In poems like "An Apple Pip" a profound emotion has driven him to write, but we do not have many experiences of which we must write. Intellectual projections such as the poems on Giacometti or after Baudelaire ("Spleen," "The Owl"), or the sonnets to Mangan, are important avenues for poetic exploration, especially for a poet of Wheatley's academic interests. In his most recent poems, a critical faculty of projection and intellectual discourse is mirrored in form, and in the decentering of the lyric 'I'.

The question of voice has been important to Wheatley since the beginning of his writing career. There has been a conscious attempt to place himself in the world, to stabilize the "I." For example, in "Sleepwalking," Wheatley writes of his own struggle, "I had seen for the first time / stripping of meaning the place that I knew / without a word or a struggle, threatening / only that it might become habitable." In "Visiting Hour," he writes of a suffering patient's "failing body that [he] loved / and placed in a stranger's hands to cure / of sickness at its very core." In each of these poems, the poetry is found in habitation and survival. The lyric voice admits the simplicity of its aims and extols the courage of its sympathy. The fragrant, nettle-stung memory of apple-picking under his grandparents' roof and care in "An Apple Pip" is openly restorative in its gesture to "give it all a second chance;

/ my long-dead grandparents restored to life . . . the windfalls falling upward to the branch." It is not merely Neo-Georgian.

If it seems in a minor vein, far from the gods and martial strain of major poetry, it is good to remember the benefits and relevance of a minor tradition in poetry. When partially surrendered to the formal necessities of meter and rhyme, the personal voice renders a particular and fundamental type of beauty which the idiosyncratic, organic form of free verse too often does not. The latter can be flatly personal or journalistic. It is not Larkin versus Pound but rather Larkin and Pound that one may aspire to exist within a poetic tradition, even if it is not possible within an individual poetic talent. The demands of formal verse may be why British and Irish poetry seem so much more consistent than American poetry, even if the latter raises a more individual type of genius under its banner of free verse as standard of individual freedom. This is not the place for sorting out these questions, but in the work of relatively young poets, such questions loom — as they have in recent years for Wheatley. Would the aesthetic of a modernist or postmodernist avant-garde be more suitable for the experience Ireland faces in the coming decade, after the decentering of Catholicism, the erosion of tradition? Poets in Ireland, from Thomas Kinsella on, have tried to answer the question, which is not easily answered. One suspects that the discussion will continue for the foreseeable future. Like his colleague at *Metre*, Justin Quinn, Wheatley himself has made the discussion particularly relevant to his own poetic growth.

In poems like the title poem of the second volume, "Misery Hill," as well as in "AM Radio," "A Garden in September," and "At a Yüan Play," there is a subtle acknowledgement made for the shift in the origins of knowledge and power, the economic urgency of the times, the broadening of cultural awareness, and for the technological age. Take the following example from "Misery Hill": "The wind lifts again, a post-office van / passes silently by with letters / for anywhere but this grim street / with its rubble and wire-topped walls, / featureless and empty besides." Perhaps a suggestion of slant rhyme, some assonance, and metrical flatness do enough to acknowledge the despair that is the poem's subject. In "AM Radio," where "The static / is the sound of the world's / axis turning," Wheatley uses the suggestion of free verse, fading in and out of meter, to capture the place of his subject, the radio, in human consciousness: "... This smooth plastic / box devours sleep, / spits dreams out // and builds invisibly, / wide and high / as the room's four walls, / its babel in the air." Similarly, in "A Garden in September," whose subject is strictly within the personal confines of the minor tradition, Wheatley adjusts his form to suggest the loss of innocence, with a fading "chalked hopscotch grid" and "the cat on the wall / picking its way more cautiously / through the scattered mosaic of jagged glass." Such formal maneuvers are achieved most fully in recent poems from *Terrestrial Variations*.

In "Riptide," "The Owl," "Macaw," "St John and the Eagle," and "Fintan and the Hawk of Achill," a dominant avian interest is made apparent, one which Wheatley shares with Caitríona O'Reilly. For both poets, birds present an image of otherness, a gothic double (as in "Macaw" where the bird echoes the poet), a moving feast of perspectives and insight. The aerial show of the war plane in "Riptide" and the mythological attribution of wisdom in "The Owl" set the stage for the other poems. In "Fintan and the Hawk of Achill," the mythological, religious, and aesthetic properties come together to define a significant part of Wheatley's forming poetic, figuring ancient Fintan as he seeks transcendence and forgiveness. Here, "one Bealtaine Eve" (roughly one summer's evening, for in the Celtic calendar Bealtaine begins in May along with the "good weather") Fintan encounters the mysteries of Irish fauna (blackbird, salmon, eagle, hawk) and landscape (the Bann, the Suir, the Liffey, the Shannon rivers), and so delves into the instinctual depths of consciousness. It is one of the most ambitious and successful poems among the most recent ones, uniting the poet's desire to experiment with form (especially line-spacing and the left-hand margin) and his most recent mythological and natural themes. "Chemical Plant" and "St. John and the Eagle," on the other hand, illustrate some other important positions that Wheatley as poet has taken in recent years. In the first poem he sets the scene, with a deliberate nod to the music of the Seventies, as well as to the environmental consciousness that was then burgeoning. He proceeds to give his modernist fragmentation of the Anglo-Saxon caesura both personal and universal significance, capturing the sources of a rock-music aesthetic and giving it poetic concision:

this chemistry we do

to feed the fire   firing the hum
that rises   snaking   from each tower
and drives   the chain reaction   home
that surges   when it finds us,   lover,
and runs to ground   through our pale flame.

Thematic and formal concerns are balanced by using enjambment and careful line spacing to suggest breaks in consciousness, and by using the traditional device of caesura to highlight the rhythm that drives the contemporary reality he is describing. In the second poem, "St John and the Eagle," natural and sacred imagery combine to threaten the position of the poet / believer / transcriber of the Word who stands below the flight of the sacred bird and watches his own emblem. Like prophets, poets seeks their truths, the word made flesh, amid the perishable world of shadows, even though they are perishable themselves. This fate awaits all who seek the "fugitive image, *imago aquilae*." For Wheatley warns us, "no sooner will you have finished / this page than talons will / puncture and carry it off." Here we have an image of why he is struggling against the constraints of formal poetry and why he is reluctant to be firmly connected with anything like "New Formalism."

The last, most experimental selection of Wheatley's work presents the form the conversation with himself and his poetic is taking. "The Truth of a Folklore Beyond Compare" is part of an ongoing dialogue; one in which Wheatley is reappraising his former poetic pose while trying to test its best themes and plumb the depths of his intellectual and musical knowledge. The poem contains insightful critical appraisal of music: "Among the most important effects on the pipes is the contrast between C natural and C sharp, as featured in so many piping tunes, Doran's version of "Rakish Paddy" for one. Consider how differently he does it on his two recordings of that track, working the regulators each time like a pack of hounds on the chanter's trail." The poem places such critical awareness alongside a fervent wish to fulfill his poetic talents: "Pipeless today, I look up as the bus passes the cemetery and wonder where I have buried my music. Sometimes he plays C natural, sometimes C sharp. How I dreamed, as a child, of the tower on the mysterious German's land behind the estate." As a critic, Wheatley is supremely aware of how mockingbird-like the poet can be, but he realizes that most poets can only dream of possessing the facility of what Whitman called "the musical shuttle." His responses are understandable efforts to broaden his range and deepen his voice. There is an admirable, if precipitous quality to his assessments. We must watch where such broadening brings the poet, as the quest is central to the future of Irish poetry.

SINÉAD MORRISSEY

Born in County Armagh in 1972, Sinéad Morrissey grew up in Belfast, and went to Trinity College, Dublin, where she studied English and German between 1990 and 1995. In 1994, she took a year out of her studies to teach in Flensburg, Germany. After completing her B.A., she lived in Japan, where she taught English, and moved on to New Zealand, living on the shores of the Waitakere Dam for a further year, before returning to Ireland in 1999. Without doubt, her education and travel have shaped Morrissey's development, but familial and personal interests have also played their part in forging a poetic of religious, intellectual and political force. In her first volume of poetry, *There was Fire in Vancouver* (1996), faith is akin to poetic insight, a gesture of belief in another person, and a fitting perspective on larger social and historical movements. The first poem of this selection tells us that Morrissey's upbringing by Communist parents, whose conviction was "too much to see through" ("Among Communists"), propelled her towards considering the nature and question of faith. Much of this consideration, in terms of poetic influence, she openly owes to R.S. Thomas, the Welsh poet who was also a cleric, both for dark doubts and meditations on the absence of God as well as for his faith, but clearly family played its part. What is important and striking in the context of Irish society, however, is how faith has become bankrupt for much of contemporary Ireland and Irish intellectuals. Fortunately, Morrissey's interest in religion never leads her to conventional statements of a simple-minded credo and is only one aspect of a rich poetic sensibility. Rather it provides a category of feeling which no other type of thinking can offer, one which has been increasing undervalued, even treated hostilely in Irish literary and cultural spheres. Without doubt, religious influence in Ireland has waned considerably, but one must remember that the new prelates (journalists, politicians, critics, even poets themselves) also have their conventions, their power bases to satisfy.

True questions of faith, like those of poetry, exist on the margins of experience and society, and on the margins of power, involving values outside the ordinary operations of daily life. Like poetry, faith is a question of perspective, even for a non-believer like Philip Larkin: "To look out once from High Windows was to fly / Over the walls you saw in life" ("To Look Out Once from High Windows"). Morrissey's poems remind us why faith as a perspective remains essential regardless of the position of organized religion or of any individual position. In the midst of poems on various subjects, the religious experience is there to arrest all presumptions of our own sacred cows, be they skeptical or holy. The title poem of her first volume, *There was Fire in Vancouver*, insists that we need a Moses to remind us not to worship the Golden Calf. Her second volume, *Between Here and There* (2002), expands her subject matter somewhat, but the essential questions are still placed between "rockhard atheism" and "prayer," as Morrissey states in the title poem "Between Here and There." In some of her most recent as yet uncollected poems, a note of anxiety, a spiritual need, continues to haunt what seems now to be an increasing confidence in her own artistic powers. She wonders is the sky "merely on fire / with its own futility" ("Polar"), while the "Angel of Anxiety" ("Contrail") hovers on the stairs. From the beginning, there has been a battle with the angels and truths that faith and knowledge impart.

Celestial and cerebral struggles have their important political and social parallels. In the early poem "Europa Hotel" (a hotel repeatedly bombed by the IRA in the worst years of the Troubles in Northern Ireland), a recent bombing affects how the young poet from Belfast views reality itself for the weeks ahead: "Your view impaired for another fortnight / Of the green hills they shatter you for." Many writers from the North have discussed the very personal effects the bombings and tit-for-tat killings have had on them. Terror changes our perspective. The very landscape takes on an historical edge. "After the Hurricane" also examines cause and effect, action and reflection. The hurricane "is the breath of God" devastating the American coastline. "There was too much rage in the sky for it not to be God's," the poet contends. For a European, the sight of an American storm must be a positively evangelical, bible-thumping experience. (Europe has a climate, the joke runs, while the United States has weather.) Again, we are standing at a window, watching "a shower of cars / Spat out like sycamore seeds," and again our perspective on the landscape, trailing "wires / In its rush to be pure," is radically altered: "You felt too temporary not to be answerable / To the power of the break up of hills." The ephemeral nature of human existence when confronting the power of a storm (or a bomb) is the basis of all religious questioning: even the permanent forms of Wordsworth's rocks, stones and trees, are subject to sweeping change.

For Morrissey, the revelatory quality of political violence is particularly imperative when we place "Europa Hotel" in the context of the volume at large. The surreal fire in "There was Fire in Vancouver" suddenly becomes more terrible, and the last line, "we watched with Moses standing in our heads," echoes from Vancouver to modern-day Jerusalem, from Belfast to Bali, from Manhattan to Baghdad, as the sense that we are watching humankind up to its old tricks again, bowing to the mark of the beast within us, is inescapable. In "Glaciers," the author of the script is addressed: "God's wand is absolute." The magic is terrifying and so, "Looking at glaciers // Jinxed into stillness," the poet fears for herself under the sway of lunar tides: "I miss oceans in my head." Gods have their messages as well as their messengers, and the poet is listening. In "My New Angels," the new angels are said to be different from the old, as the difficulty of our age requires. The "old angels made us peaceful," Morrissey insists. God's new angels will be wrathful rather than merciful: "My new angels are howling, hard . . . Their rage is assured, ragged, unforgiving. / There is no perfecting them." A sin exists, a "snuffed out light on a back road," for which we have to pay. The evangelical is no simple-minded messenger of good news in Morrissey's poetry, for she is no fundamentalist. The city of God, as she writes in "Monteverdi's Vespers," is a "City compacted in faith and damage."

We have broken the covenant, but accepting that, and looking up, we may be like Larkin at the end of her poem to him: "You have stopped your various desolations colliding / By just looking up. You built your runway out of decimated love / And saw in flight how nothing could be left to lose or prove." The scene is often apocalyptic in her first volume, and the birds, promising flight, escape or transcendence, are messengers themselves. Perhaps "the cry of the gulls accompanies you with knowledge" ("Monteverdi's Vespers"); our relationship to the truths of the world around us is as primitive as ever, for we still look to the animal world for analogy. In "The Juggler," the artist becomes a figure out of our folkloric past: an "anachronism" who "puts the clock back / Nine hundred years" and who forces us to watch him, we who feel "the drain / Of things modern." The "spinning blue arc" of the juggling act becomes both like the act of creation itself and the act of surviving within its unknowable, unalterable, and unforgiving laws. "Natural begrudgers," writes Morrissey,

We are nevertheless caught

By the weightlessness, the controlled
Mechanics of air

With all the improbables cajoled
Into truth[.]

From the view of the juggling act afforded by the violence of the hurricane in Florida as well as by the bomb in Northern Ireland, she can credibly state: "we are not as far out / From faith as we were."

In the next volume, *Between Here and There,* the political and sacred violence of the first volume either moves to the background or takes more artistic, personal shape ("Sea Stones"). The personal and artistic natures of the meditation in this volume predominate, and questions concerning the origins of knowledge become central. In "Jo Gravis in His Metal Garden," works of art have metaphysical applications. The garden is Edenic, at least inferentially, but it is also earthly; the "signs" which surround the artist seem of particular importance in the poem, calling the inanimate world to life, giving meaning where in a technological or metal age none seems to lie, creating "a lullaby / to flesh in a fleshless gallery." In many poems, signs are meant to be hidden ("Zero Visibility"), appreciated if not possessed ("Our Flower Garden") or else mourned ("Stitches"). In "An Anatomy of Smell," such signs are not visible but rather olfactory and they are "giveaways of origin." From the familial smells attached to children at school ("one was made of wine; one walked crushed by blankets even under the sun") to the lovers of adulthood ("the hidden nature of the generative act"), these olfactory signs carry their own secret identity. With them, we establish the "identity" of the individual life, the social unit. The poem concludes: "When we move house / such genealogies as these will follow us." If one had thought that the poet had radically altered the nature of her song, closer examination reveals this not to be the case.

Different, but related philosophical issues of perspective unsettle the poet's consciousness in the poems concerning Japan. In "Night Drive in Four Metaphors," truth is found more in metaphor than in actuality: "A moon on its back under the shadow of its circle is a unique moon. / It means home is under the weight of a stone and the brightness can come from under a shadow." In "Between Here and There," the Buddha of Nara as an icon of faith is undercut by the worldly ambition of its worshippers to house it in the "biggest wooden building in the world." The Buddha is meant to be a great religious icon of transcendence and being ("His crossing was a falling into light"); nevertheless, Nagaswa's bold claim to chant souls to Paradise through the worship of the Buddha is weakened by the notion that they first have to live within his parish —that is, between here and Ogaki. In "Goldfish," we are told that the "philosophers / wanted about them so much gold underwater to tell them what waited / in another element like breathing water. We are immediately reminded of the theme of "Awaiting Burial." Now the religious spirit is more Zen than Christian, and we are told that "closing eyes is to see." In the surprising poem "To Imagine an Alphabet," Buddhist imagery stands among the impressionistic effects of Japanese painting. Though it is an animal of Buddhist tradition, the stag resonates in Western readers' minds with Christian symbolism. Ultimately, the poem moves between the signs of various cultures, trying to uncover some fundamental substrata that link them all. Grammar, like reality, or landscape, is blurred in the process. In the end, after "murder comes," there appears a vision of a "terrible stag, flames shooting from his heart, as he prepares to walk and preach."

Rather than discussing the place of faith itself, Morrissey increasingly attempts to present an image of its fury and oppressiveness. She is acutely aware of the dangers which attend faith's intersection of epistemology and culture. This is particularly true of her newest poems. "Flight" describes a woman who is martyred for speaking her mind, and whose sufferings make the sacred iconography of her day pale when placed beside the image of her silencing with a "tongue of iron": "Christmas consumes its own bright fire / And blazes by its absence. There is too much law / To live by, and I have torn my face / In two by swallowing silence." The title of "Zero" refers to the number that Alexander the Great borrowed from the Babylonians. The Greeks were resistant to this abstract concept, concentrating instead on geometry at which they excelled. Because zero was not adopted into mainstream Western mathematics until much later, the Western world lagged behind the East. The poem "Pilots" looks at a pod of whales who have found their way into Belfast Lough. The natural world takes on the significance of her many themes: environmental because they have swum into the pollution of the nuclear reactor at Sellafield; religious, because of the wonder they elicit; and figurative, for the whales are like new-found lands whose discovery becomes a sublime emblem that transcends speech.

Taken from an aid to anatomy students by Paracelsus (Theophrastus Philippus Aureolus Bombastus von Hohenheim, 1493–1541, famous for his "bombastic" ideas about healing, faith and knowledge), "The Wound Man" contains many of her recurrent themes and presents a multivalent text. In this poem to Federico García Lorca, an image of New York after the collapse of Wall Street in 1929 and before World War II, is tied to the collapse of the Twin Towers of the World Trade Center. Angels seem to fly around the monumental figure of the wound man, who strides through the city streets: "A knife in the cheek; an arrow in the thigh." Morrissey wonders what Lorca would think had he survived all the wars and the "fall of faith," not only faith in entire systems of living, shattered twice over with the Wall-Street crash of 1929 and September 11, 2001, but even faith in ourselves. She then presents the Wound Man, "walking, tall and imperious, / through the streets of America, surly and muscular." Is it some merciful incarnation or the wrathful Second Coming? He is "Loose in the world. And out of proportion." He seems to be there just to be wounded: "There are weapons through every part of him." Nevertheless, he strides like Yeats's rough beast, preparing for vengeance. If Morrissey's faith is being tested, so is ours, and by the very weapons we have created. The Wound Man, the embodiment of the rationale for war, must continue to stalk us, if only to endure our attacks and to retaliate — for having been hurt, he must make all suffer. With such an ability to capture the present predicament, the years ahead should prove highly formative to a poet of Morrissey's interests and talents, which is auspicious for poetry, if not very prophetic of good things to come.

CAITRÍONA O'REILLY

Born in 1973, Caitríona O'Reilly grew up in County Wicklow and studied English and Archaeology at Trinity College, Dublin, where she wrote her Ph.D. on American poetry (specifically Emily Dickinson, H.D., and Sylvia Plath), commencing what would be formative poetic dialogues with the tradition. Much like her predecessors' poetry, hers can be alternately unflinchingly personal and sculpturally objective as occasion demands. One of her main themes is how the rational mind discovers the primitive darkness and orders the impending chaos. Dickinson is of particular prominence in these inheritances, as are H.D. and Plath; however, O'Reilly regards the self-justifying female egoism of some of Plath's poetry more equivocally. Her reluctance to write about herself has led her not to write very directly about people. For her, Dickinson's oblique angle on truth is exemplary. She seems intent on stripping away all humanist presumptions concerning the non-human or animal world. Nevertheless, she has a strongly sympathetic poetic, for the virtues and vices of human intelligence are very much her subject. The creatures inhabiting her world are at once familiar and strange to us, like those uncanny images that rise from our subconscious. In this, her training as an archeologist has served her well, even if the depths or heights she scales are often underwater or in the air as well as below the ground. She is constantly seeking the angle on the object which will make it hang fire, trying to capture some original focus or discovery of being — a first infatuation with reality, a flame burning in a secret place, an eye and a mode of seeing which is not ours, which we have only partially experienced, but which suddenly deepens our insight. One might wonder at an Irish poet so removed from more conventional Irish contexts such as history or politics. O'Reilly does not avoid these issues, as several of the poems in this anthology make clear, but she does consistently relate them to the processes of perception, to observation of experience and nature. As a result, any general deliberation of her work must begin and end with close reading, responding to the terms of the poems themselves, and opening discussion of any particular poem rather than limiting it. It is not necessarily true of other poets' work (and is not a value judgment) where the contexts are more definitely drawn. When O'Reilly's verbal skills find their themes, the results are textual rather than contextual. She works with assurance, avoiding the colloquial, insisting that the powers of poetry must do their work, until, as in the poem "On a Dropped Feather," language is let fly and finally becomes something else, unveiling the origins of form itself.

O'Reilly's debut collection, *The Nowhere Birds* (2001), grows in strength as the volume progresses. It charts the maturation of a poet. Many of the earlier poems are concerned with childhood and adolescence, while the later poems are more self-conscious, philosophical and widely traveled. At her best, O'Reilly creates poems of an impersonal, indeed intellectual variety. For instance, the conclusion (and even the title) of her poem "Marmoreal" contains this difference from the familiar: "from the howling circle, we'll stare / in silence from our stone address. // Two eyeless statues under snow / blinded by their own bodies' whiteness." These lines move through Eiléan Ní Chuilleanáin's "Pygmalion's Image" back to Mallarmé's *symboliste* resistance to the values of the quotidian. Even personal themes are best explored when employing such resistance: "The windows opposite might well have caught / her white divided face as she proved herself just // narrow enough to step clear, as from her own bones. / He'd wonder where she was when he got home" ("They Do It with Mirrors"). The man's confusion upon his return home echoes contemporary problems of family, selfhood and place. "Sunday" presents the issue of rampant commercial construction in the heart of Dublin without any tedious overt commentary, while also exploring questions of identity. A line from Beckett's novel *Molloy* best describes the particular accomplishments of O'Reilly's poetic: "To restore silence is the role of objects." The restoration of the silence, and with it the restoration of the object, is the aim of many post-war Irish writers from 1960 to 1990, many of whom are devotees of Beckett. For O'Reilly, this goal is partly achieved through a formal silencing of personal voice. In "Cedar of Lebanon," the object is presented in a primeval pose, hovering over the pit of chaos from which it was born:

The original metaphor
has become the last

that had a deltic beginning
that was fragrant
leaf-lipped and vermilion

casts its shadow momently
on the floor of the pit [.]

This short poem is an audacious Poundian meditation on the thing itself, full of the microscopic eye, natural curiosity ("leaf-lipped"), and specific learning ("deltic beginning") which characterizes so much of the best of O'Reilly's poetry. The cedar of Lebanon is a fitting emblem of such an object: it is known for its durability; it is connected to the foundation and pillars of Solomon's temple, to the incorruptible virtues of Christ's flesh; and, as is alluded to in the first lines, it is nearly extinct in its native country. The poem does exceptional work at the restoration of the silence (and object) that Beckett had mandated. The air of the archaic hovers near her work ("momently"), insisting on the arcane bookish quality of deep knowledge, even if such knowledge is experientially garnered from time spent observing in the fields. Likewise, we are assured that, for this poet, poetry has its own epistemology; and its tools, in this case metaphor, are oracular as no other form of understanding can be.

"The Cedar of Lebanon" and "Marmoreal" have set a high standard that O'Reilly's best poems, especially her most recent, consistently meet. In the two sonnets, "On a Dropped Feather" and "Augury" (the latter closing her first volume), the poet's powers become vividly apparent. Her voice is consistently striking and original. Words, vital in their context, accumulate meaning, and rub against unusual scientific and naturalistic terms. Her sense of the object world as the chief method of uncovering layers of perception has deepened considerably since the publication of her first volume. The animals that move through her poems, particularly birds and fishes, almost take the place of people, as well as of the Other, of the inhuman opposite that most deeply questions our assumptions and perspectives. The best poems endeavor to reestablish consciousness in the face of what threatens its extinction. O'Reilly is part of a larger movement in Irish literature (including John Montague, Seamus Heaney, Paula Meehan, Seán Lysaght, Vona Groarke and John McGahern) toward examining nature and landscape on their own terms as well as historical documents of conquest and dispossession. Examination on these terms has been part of nature writing in the United States for some time: "Wilderness is a civilization other than our own," Henry David Thoreau famously stated. In O'Reilly, the civilization that nature constitutes, instead of merely presenting the unfathomable and obscurely barbaric heart of darkness, actually holds the key to our deepest symbols: "We wonder how will the river change . . . who will watch its black dreams / shatter into figments / skulled and crossboned in light ("The River," the first section of "Six Landscapes"). In the next section, entitled "Littoral," O'Reilly shows how consciousness slowly and almost inarticulately comes to terms with its environments, to a sufficing image of some kind, employing a seven-syllable verse form (to match the seven stones, in a Pythagorean harmony of numbers) that relies on simile rather than metaphor, on likenesses rather than pure associations, in order to unfold its "ostrich-egg of granite" along the shore. Here we move from the "slate grey mood" of Ireland and cultural consciousness of the I.R.A. to an acceptance of the desolate scene through formal adherence to detail.

In later sections of the above sequence, consciousness and the natural world also redefine each other in forceful ways: "Down the darkening cinder-path, fenced at both ends, / their children's voices cry to me like owls" ("The Avenues"). Here, in the Swiftian tradition, the lines between the natural and human worlds are blurred. In other parts of the sequence, they inform one another more vigorously: "In Caspe, light pours through the gap // the hills create in being at odds / with each other against the flaming sky" ("In Aragón"). The poem shows how nature, culture and landscape are interlinked. O'Reilly emphasizes how we view the Spanish landscape as we view the Spanish themselves. This connection between culture and landscape is equally true of the Irish, of course, as in "Uggool," a poem on an eponymous place near Clare Island in Co. Mayo: "It was only when the road ended / and the engine stopped ticking / that we noticed the silence / that was of space unfolding / and ourselves absorbed by it, / unburdened by the light's extension." Later poems continue to enforce the theme of the mind's interaction with a natural scene or animal occurrence: "black butterflies / brushing their wings against my mind's ceiling" ("Poliomyelitis"). In "Lag," O'Reilly discovers a movement so deeply intricate that it threatens to vanquish self-perception in the complex workings of a vine around a tree: "What lapses from an eye not quick enough to see / ivy hooking itself to a tree / how the numb foliage explodes?" Her minute examination of subject-object relations, her willingness to capture annihilation of consciousness, to almost invite it, has both risks and rewards. The attempt in "Duets," mirrored in art and song, has its own "gothic hollowness" while crossing "its own vast space."

In "Gravitations," a central Newtonian principle slowly becomes a relative one under the combined weight of deep inspection and introspection. In other poems like "The Maze," consciousness itself becomes a labyrinth one cannot escape: "I never remember the road, / though I take it nightly. Each night . . . new pathways open to terminate / like shut valves or lopped thoracic branches, / nowhere." The question becomes urgent in "X-Ray," in which the subject becomes an absolutely passive spectator undergoing treatment, like the ideal spectator before the operation of the world. It is an act of ancient, almost sexual significance much like those saintly experiences of mystic union with God. "I am lain against the plate," O'Reilly writes, deliberately using a contextualized archaism in order to hint at sexual passiveness and relinquishment of the self: "A thrown shadow dissects / the self from what it was." This dissection of the self could mean a new beginning or a complete end. "Can flesh become all shadow?" she asks. She answers with a concise, natural analogy: "Not yet: as through a glass / brightly and fragile as a bird's / shine my long blue bones." She has begun to think like a mountain, to think objectively, to listen to the wolf's howl, to watch the birds" flight, to see herself upon the table, with the same passive wisdom as the land views the life that takes place upon it. Her own fragility is the reason she can fly. O'Reilly is looking for the objective correlative of the poetic imagination. In "Floater," she finds it in those shape-changing objects floating in our eyes which we catch in our vision; it is a "caddis-case from which (invisibly) some brisk beast fled."

Nature is her "labyrinthine Gospel," where she may "gild the Virgin's Mantle" ("Pollen") and watch how the bee "dusts his muscular back." Yet, she knows that if nature is read scripturally, it must need redemption. The beautiful "A Quartet for the Falcon" celebrates the life and vision of the raptor, aware of the bird's power in flight, its beauty and its deadly skills. And it does not forget how alike the human and inhuman mind can be, for all of their sentimental differences: "Over a bleached Segovian plain the eye / seeks its eagle like the sky's pupil." The effort to unveil the source of perspective, of vision, "describe[s] a brutal circle." The impersonal demands of true insight are made of hard material: "tear-drop and cut diamond." Finally, all efforts and demands come down to scrutinizing the fall from grace, the mark of the beast. The beast must be lured with the symbols of savage fate and consumption: "now her sentimental silhouette descends / to a swung horseshoe bound in leather. / It is the World, the Flesh, the Devil" ("The Lure"). One might suspect that there is a disembodied form of Puritanism driving these reflections. There is little sensual life experienced by the poet beyond her mere witnessing of the sensual wonders of the world. Her purifying drive comes at an unusual time in Irish history, when change has been so broad and rapid. O'Reilly seems less worried about historical contexts than testing the philosophical texture of perception itself. The old concepts of Ireland are nearly exhausted. She argues that we should return from concept to percept, from formulated conventions and ideas to the sensual apprehensions of the world around us, and see what this staging ground may have to tell us. There is doubtless some form of Puritanism at work here. Perhaps this explains O'Reilly's affection for American poets, especially Dickinson, H.D. and Plath, who had their own struggles with purification and corruption in similarly transitional stages in their country's history. Poetry is ridding itself of everything that is not concerned with poetic perception, impersonal and self-mortifying. Caitríona O'Reilly's efforts to look at the changing world with new eyes are ambitious, even historic, at this pivotal period in Ireland.

ACKNOWLEDGMENTS

Wake Forest University Press warmly acknowledges the particular generosity of the artist Patrick Scott and the Taylor Galleries of Dublin for the artwork on the cover of this anthology.

All the poets have been of invaluable assistance in the creation of this anthology, for which I am very appreciative.

I would also like to express gratitude to Nicole Guippone and Meghan McGuire for their diligent editorial efforts.

Candide Jones deserves special mention for her indefatigable work and support as colleague and devotee of poetry, as does Dillon Johnston, the founder of WFU Press, for playing his advisory role with his usual insight and finesse.

And, as always, I thank Wanda Balzano for her inspiration and editorial help. Of course, any mistakes herein are solely my responsibility.

Jefferson Holdridge, Winston-Salem, NC 2005

Harry Clifton

The Waking Hour

Riddled with contradictions, the waking hour
Is upon us, and everywhere about us
Morning, the sense of existence
And the three dimensions
Coming together, whitening pillows and walls.

And I float upwards, from my own depths,
With a woman beside me
Wondering, wondering am I real
Or an angel trapped in the glass of a bedside prayer
And have I come into her life, and will I stay there

With the other objects, nailed to the wall
Like permanence, or habit,
Achieving humanity, averaging out
Between sacred and profane, through the long attritions
Marriage and work ordain. . . .

Deliver us, Lord, from the loss of intensity
Now, as on every day
Of heightened beginnings, that pass away
With the first word spoken, the earliest bird
To strike a false note

Or the city announcing itself
In klaxons and white noise, delivering
To our disembodied selves
Wherever we are, the temporal fruits
Of Eden, the past and future again.

The Walls of Carthage

Augustine, ended the priest,
Put it all too well.
Here am I, a priest
In my late forties, still

In the desert, still
Relativity's fool.
Wherever it is the will
Of *lycée*, college, school,

As here, God to conclude
From premisses, I am sent
For lectures, *journées d'études*.
Oases of discontent,

Paris, Maynooth, Louvain,
Define my forty-year desert,
My home from home, terrain
Of groundless visions, assert

The same topography
As he, Augustine, mapped.
Godless in Carthage city,
A dialectician, trapped

In a waste of comparisons,
His speech is my speech, speech
Of failure, of a man
Old enough now to preach

Of a God he may never know
Under the sun — mirage.
So, with Augustine I tell you,
Alexandria, Carthage,

We, in inferior reason,
Travel until we fall,
To compare, in a desert season,
The beauty of their walls.

Office of the Salt Merchant

Once in a while,
I have wished to see more than the head
Of that girl who smiles,
Disembodied, behind bloodred

Service hatches. . . .
I wanted her hands,
From which a visiting merchant detaches
Yellow and white invoices, to extend,

As if in kindness to myself,
Pale salt in graded rows
Of crucibles along the empty shelf
Of the sales window,

Where I might see the atmosphere change
Her anaemic samples
As I did before, and stay once more in the range
Of a common example.

The Desert Route

Exempted from living, abandoned
To some infinite fascination he has
With a gentle goat by a wall,
Here where the trade routes start

The idiot sits, clad in the cast-offs
Of a town full of tailors,
Unembarrassed
By any such thing as self.

Around him in chaos, preparations
For the desert . . . camels genuflecting
To necessity, loaded with iron bedsteads,
Struggling to rise; and donkeys

With lank, hopeless penises,
Jesuit eyes,
Marking time.
In time they all set out,
Like free beings, across a desert

He will never go through again, relieved
Of space and time
To be lost in. Doesn't even notice
How everything still moves outwards

To the same end . . . the camel trains,
The slow asphalting-gangs
On the superhighway, laying down
Lines of purpose, almost merging

At times, almost parallel,
Except at the border, where a soldier
With three stripes, wishing himself elsewhere
Is waving the landrovers on.

The Vultures

Imagine that smell
On the high escarpment, forty miles from town,
Where eighty donkeys fell
In the Rainy Season . . . how can I walk and disown,

Around here, what the vultures do?
Called Health Inspectors,
Legalised, like beautiful African avenues,
African slums, death and protection

Incarnate in the same
Untouchables . . . Under their wing
I see how the leprous and maimed
Turned professional beggar, how minor tragedies cling,

Repeat themselves
From tribesman to tribesman —civilised diseases,
Prophylactic shelves
Of Medicine Men, Mahomet in scuffles with Jesus

Tonight on the autumn streets
As Rhamadan ends. . . .
Upstaging their African roots
At the Hotel Terminus, the Sahara All Stars Band

Is tuning up. I pity the prostitute,
Deprived of name and culture,
Whose life is a first floor room there, a free cigarette
When the buses arrive. I envy the code of the vulture

Who followed the tribes into town
Like a memory, a past into which elders rot
As the Rains die down
And the New Moon shines. They've laid the dead within earshot

Of evening prayers, in ultraviolet rays
From amplified mosques. Ironic sophistication —
Catarrhine faces
Streaming with catarrh . . . No further dispensation,

Now, for the sons to fulfil,
To carry their own dead fathers
On their backs, back into the obsolete hills
Where vultures still gather.

Trial Marriage

Listening, woman and man,
To a solitary drunk in the passage, his key out of place,
Or the rhythm of an old fan
In the darkness, chasing itself through space

Above our heads . . . is the government paying
For them too? It's casual as a universe
To keep cold in, this living with charges reversed
And our credit weakens, as the hotel moves into day.

When the nets are lifted
We slept under, and we're posted separate ways —
After months of arrogance, among beauty parlour facelifts,
Sad divorcées — I'll be scouring for days

A memory of pure flesh
From idle fingers. Nobody's shame or disgrace . . .
Am I free to exploit you afresh
In a marriage of words? The meaning behind your face,

Your hands' competence, anyway these prevail
Elsewhere than in words. From the first of our pleasure
You said of your long fingernails,
Too long for mending and tearing, 'Too much leisure . . .'

After the trial marriage, trial separations —
I hate them, the working selves we're paid to assume,
Transferred to indifferent stations, our working conditions
Never look back, simply resume.

Latitude 5°N

A forest of background noises,
African classroom . . . Voices emerge from it,
Angry voices of children, whose names
I cannot decipher, demanding
Euclidean instruments, Oxford dictionaries,
Chairs of native wood
For their growing fundaments. Answering,
Drowned in the din of a construction gang
Levelling ground outside, I repeat myself,
Beseeching silence.

Or again, the night
Of the open forum . . . A forest of background noises
Planting itself in the crowd
Of black contemporaries, filibustering
The maiden speeches of girls
With shouts from the assembly. The MC drops
His faulty megaphone, imploring
Silence, but a man with a powerful voice,
Denouncing Western culture
Has the floor.

The Catholic father, drunk
And disillusioned . . . 'Give us religious war
All over again —the privilege of suffering,
Comradeship and martyrdom . . .
Oppress us, like the church in Eastern Europe,
Where you can't postpone religion
The way we do,
Just to go on a weekend spree. Above all,
Keep us here in Africa. Never send us home
Where we have no meaning.'

Sitting in the jungle, engine ticking over,
Thinking all this... No forest of background noises
To distract me, no radio drummers
Nationalising the airwaves
For a blood revival... Nothing but silence
Five degrees from the equator —
Silence of growth, before growth
Proliferates into desires; and the agelessness
Of the man with no birth certificate,
Innocent of history.

Magyar Coat

Before I could walk, I was wheeled —
Felt vaguely eternal, Mother behind me a mystery
Out of the shadow of whose magyar coat I crawled,
Started making history.

Granny confused me, embittered
By ceaseless politics. Mother changed religion
In the Cold War, and my vague eternity shattered —
It must have been about then.

Behind long hair, dark glasses,
I hid myself, a student walking the streets
Of East Berlin, a child of the privileged classes,
Trying to make opposites meet.

The prostitutes in the lights
Of the motor showrooms, along Potsdamerstrasse
Kept their hours, from afternoon into night,
As back to the West I passed

Amid human confusion —
Coated like magyars, women of yesteryear
Swarmed in the Eastern Sector, Mother's old fashions —
The world must be going nowhere. . . .

'. . . Your magyar coat, your magyar coat,
What did I want to say? . . . Oh nothing, some nonsense . . .'
Granny is pestering Mother. It sticks in my throat,
Like trying to explain my presence

By an image, at history's
Real checkpoints, checkpoints I can't circumvent —
Where nonsense was good enough for eternal mystery,
I want to be sure what is meant.

Military Presence, Cobh 1899

Childhood. A door wide open, day or night
Without fear of trespass, as long as the tides
Gentled Her Majesty's Navy . . . why not forget
It was a year of many suicides?

Everything else being equal, you are a child
In a casual doorway, feeding naïve plums
To the suddenly orphaned . . . somebody's father files
Past into oblivion, pressganged, a Cherrybum

Bound for the colonies. Corpses are carted back
From the place below, dredged from a deepwater quay
To haunt imagination; all you lack
Is consciousness, judgement, the twentieth century.

Monsoon Girl

In the airconditioned drone
Of a room we rent by the hour,
You go to the telephone,
Lovely and naked, to put through a call
For drinks, or hire a car
To take us home.

Your nudity dapples the walls
With shadows, and splashes the mirrors
Like a vision, in the blue light
That bathes you, a pleasure-girl
On a lost planet, sincere
But only at night.

Outside, it will rain
For weeks, months on end. . . .
We'll come here again
As we did before, where Chinese women,
Blank and inscrutable, attend
Nightly to our linen.

We'll come again
In drunkenness, for the child's play
Of lovemaking, or to part the rain
Like curtains of jet beads,
And dream the rainy months away
On pampered beds

Where forgetfulness lies down
With executive power
After hours, in a tangle of legs
And juices, a world turned upside down,
And I feed on the lotus-flower
Of your delicate sex.

At three, we'll be driven back
Through depths of Bangkok
Already tomorrow. There will be roads
Closed, and a dope squad
Flashing its query through windowglass,
Letting us pass. . . .

There will be lights
In Chinatown, sampans on the river —
The poor starting early. Elsewhere the night
Will separate us, having seeded within you
Miscarriage of justice forever,
And the rain will continue.

The Seamstress

I have a seamstress, making a shirt for me
In sultry weather, in the months we are together.

She measures my shoulders with tape, I feel on my back
The cool of her wooden yardstick, and submit

To a temporary contract, binding me
To the new and the strange. Together we lose ourselves

Among shades of blue, the melancholy feast
A culture of silkworms creates, as Chinese tailors

Stand and wait. For me, it's the stuff of dreams,
For her a labour of love. . . . In her house on stilts

Where women are still slaves, she sews the collarless
Garment of pure freedom I have asked for

When I leave, keeping only for herself
Dry tailor's chalk, and the diagram of a body.

Death of Thomas Merton

Losing altitude, you can see below you the flames
Of the Tet Offensive, giving the lie to your visions
Of Eastern mystics, like uncensored newsreel
In which the slaves of history are spreading the blame —
And so your mind records it, a sin of omission
In a mystic journal. Meanwhile the wheels
Descend for Bangkok, with one of the Catholic great,
In late October, Nineteen Sixty Eight.

A clean declaration. One a.m. and you're through
The bulletproof glass of security, like a conscience
Filtered through judgement, leaving behind
Temptations you were dead to, years ago —
Hippies frisked for heroin, women and incense
For the American soldiers. Only the life of the mind
You hide on your person — all the rest you can shed
Like a stale narcotic. Shortly, you'll be dead.

So wake before daylight, breakfast alone,
Remembering what you came for. Below you a river
Seeps out of Buddhist heartlands, not in meditation
But in commerce, irrigating zones
Of military fleshpots, where the barges deliver
Rice and Thai girls, and a drifting vegetation
Drags at the chains of destroyers, moored in Bangkok —
And you wait to be chauffeured, at nine o'clock,

To the other side of the city. . . .
Spiritual masters
Shrunken to skin and bone, await you in silence
On a neutral ground of Buddhas, golden and hollow,
Smiling from inner space, beyond disaster
To an old complacency. Starving for non-violence
In saffron robes, their shavenheaded followers
Beg on the streets. From an airconditioned car
You can see them in passing, as cut off as you are —

Cut off from each other, disconnected by history
In Paris and Calcutta, linked alone by the airspace
Of a temporal pilgrimage. Diplomatic immunity,
This is your saving grace — to restore mystery
To a common weal, and resurrect from disgrace
The nonpolitical, kneeling in the unity
Of a moment's prayer, with the Dalai Lama and wife —
For the flash-photographers of *Time* and *Life*.
Judas has other betrayals. At your last supper
In a Hungarian restaurant, among friends in Bangkok,
It's left to the Chinese waiter to overprice you —
So unworldly. You can switch from corruption
Suddenly into wisdom, through an electric shock
Turning your hair white, resolving your crisis
Into anticlimax. But it leaves you dead,
With a powerline shortcircuited through your head. . . .

A small embarrassment, for the United States —
Your motherhouse at Gethsemani awaits
Its anti-hero. A gaggle of monks are released
To New Haven for the day, to identify and separate
Among the Vietnam dead, the maimed in crates
From an Air Force plane, this body of a priest
And holy fool —from beyond the international
Dateline, and the jungle war with the irrational.

Euclid Avenue

after Hart Crane

The blazing stanchions and the corporate lights —
Manhattan over the bridge, from Brooklyn Heights —
Were energies like yours, without a home,
That would not be condensed inside a poem

But endlessly dispersed, and went to work
For time and money, hovering over the masses
Like terrible angels. . . . Now, I stand in New York
And watch those energies sweat themselves out, like gases

Through a subway grille, to keep the derelicts warm
In a new depression. Or, at station bookstalls,
Calm at the eye of the electric storm
I drink your words, like prohibition alcohol

Capital hides from itself. On soundless trains
Through Middle America, citizens fishing in creeks
That rise and flow nowhere, disappear again
In a private wilderness you were born to seek

And lose yourself in. But none of them will thank you —
They, nor the desolate children that they raised
On a thousand streets called Euclid Avenue
For travelling inwards, damning with faint praise

The forces that they freed, to blast through gravity
Into a loveless, extraterrestrial space
Like night bus stations, galaxies of strays —
The sons and daughters of the human race.

Absinthe at New Orleans

America, your poisons and elixirs
    I drink by the glass
On Bourbon Street, and watch the winter pass.
An hour before dinner, the temperature hovers at sixty
Like perfection, neither hot nor cold,
And the tapdancers, thinking on their feet,
Are back on their beats. A child of Europe, I drink
The essence of wormwood, greenish, bittersweet,
And look at yesterday's slaves, the bought and sold,
And wonder at this freedom to travel and think

The State Department pays for. *Feeling alone?*
    You can always telephone
Our special number in Washington, free of charge.
We know you're out there somewhere, a conscience at large
In the privileged states. For you, distinguished guest,
Hotels are booked, there are alter egos to meet
Among the civil servants, disarmingly nice,
Who show you Death Row, *agreeing when you protest.*
About your dark side, too, we can be discreet
And omni-tolerant. Everyone has a price

In the cities we've raised. . . . A week ago
    I saw them shovelling snow
Off Omaha pavements, in an arctic breeze —
The disinherited Africans, the wizened Vietnamese
In coldweather clothing. As he paid the toll
And drove me to the airport, from my graduate class
In the politics of modern poetry,
Kurt Helmut Schroeder, working in Riot Control,
Looked at them coldly, and then looked at me,
'*There is no poverty here — only laziness!*'

Approaching Denver, gradually losing height,
    I imagined a city
Out of green smog and buildings, a hundred miles away
As we made our descent. I would sleep that night
With the Void for company, sirens, breaking glass,
And shouts below of illegal Spanish and blacks
Who left their souls behind, at the point of entry,
To be officially no one here, to hustle on East Colfax —
And businessmen, from Hiltons of steel and glass,
Who hurried in groups towards the invisible centre

Of a town with no after hours. . . . They had booked me through,
    The government, on the silver and blue
Amtrak, through to the Pacific side
Of whatever was missing here. On the Great Divide
Were failed utopias, desolate heavens on earth
A soldier on leave got down at, met by a girl —
And blizzards fumed under station lamps in the cold,
And voices of porters, urgent as death and birth,
Recalled me from the platform, where I strolled
Examining snowflakes, tiny, complete as worlds

At midnight in Salt Lake City. *Lie on the bed*
    The African steward prepares
At body temperature. Know the government cares
Beyond space and time, as you sleep through watersheds
And wake to a conscienceless desert, replacing the dark
With auto wreckage, chapels for divorcées,
Nevada bombsites —all the fossilised fishes
Of a post-historic sea. Change before Reno, at Sparks,
And cross the stateline. Quickly, forget all these,
For the bed we have made for you now, fulfills all wishes

In San Francisco. . . . Yes, I see what you mean
  About everyone having a side.
In blue December, the month of suicides,
I saw the drugged in doorways, the sadness of queens,
From an old Chinese hotel on Geary Street,
And mornings brought me unofficial news
That pulsed like pleasure, through the affective centres —
Blonde Saskatchewan girl, between my sheets,
Who never told me who it was had sent her
To compromise me, and to be my Muse.

America, the electric cablecars
  Along Saint Charles
Will carry me back, in another hour or two,
To the last hotel before Europe. . . . Meanwhile, the blues
And Dixieland jazz, the salesmen of joy and despair
At every corner —like me, *poètes maudits*,
Imbibing essence of wormwood, bittersweet —
And the steady Trades, the temperate gulf air
Emancipating crowds onto the streets
And winter, going unnoticed, everywhere.

Watershed

On the spine of Italy
Our train had come to a standstill.

Windows were pulled down
As the temperature rose

And the passengers, heatstruck,
Swatted at clouds of minor irritation.

What was this shadowless station
We were stranded in,

All wind and grasses, the blue whisper
Of alfalfa, growing wild

In a deserted summer
There was no one left to harvest?

They were ours, the abandoned houses,
Ours for the asking,

Like work, or marriage,
Or any ancient principle

Europe forgot, up here in the mountains.
I saw no rivers, starting

In either direction,
No past, no future —

Only a watershed, bearing in
With the weight of the present moment,

Transfiguring us, as we slept
In the shade of our great newspapers

With which we had beaten to death
The gadfly of remembrance.

Meltwater

Somewhere behind all this
I sense the glacier, permanently cold,
We must get back to, at any price,
For the knowledge it withholds
Like a tongue of ice

Translated in green water
Melting. . . . Call it tears
Or semen, a bottle of juniper brandy
Or the distillations of years.
O my wife, whose daughter

Are you — one of the Fates?
Yours is a nameday no one celebrates
In these mountains. Disinherited
Like me, do you love or hate?
Long enough, you have turned into spirit

Juniper berries, straining their seeds
Through meshes of muslin, pickled quinces
For the sweetness they bleed,
And made intensity, measured it out
In fluid ounces.

Long enough, you have cried,
'I remember so little,' into your pillow
And wished you might have died.
Your face was an eddy that tears had blorted,
Ecstasy distorted,

While I swam above you
Looking down, through the waters
Between us, so terrifyingly clear,
That we drink from here —

I, who love you.
Pack your bags. We can start
For the black depressions, drizzling crags
Where the work of the heart
Is accomplished. Miles of tracks
Lead in and back

To what feels like childhood
Already, where to walk is to retrace,
Like babes in the wood,
The steps of avalanche victims
Foetal in ice.

Heterae

Towards daybreak, I dreamt again
Of long ago and far away.
A woman, one of the heterae
I had known in a former life,
Was ageing on an endless train.
Asleep beside me, my wife

Kept her own dark rendezvous
With revenants and private ghosts,
Alternatives that rose in hosts
Articulating the unsaid —
Ancestral voices, coming through
From the lives she might have led.

The heterae, the heterae —
I am back again, one autumn day
By a Paris underground station
Awaiting Her, the gorgeous flirt
Who jilts without explanation
Foolish spirits. But no one is hurt.

I wake again, in a barn by the Nore
One winter morning, seeing frost
In spicules on the windowpane,
Ethereal, starlike, galaxies lost
And never to be seen again —
The morning after the night before,

She shifts her body, throws her leg
Companionably over mine,
A Wexford girl, who herds the cattle
Trampling snow outside our door.
Easygoing as Queequeg
She feeds me sexual lore.

I wander the world, I return —
Lose myself, again and again,
Inside a woman, take the cure,
A restless child, with his fingers burnt
By stolen beauty, stolen fire,
Dreaming faces, endless trains . . .

The heterae, the heterae —
Feckless, inconstant,
Glorying in the instant,
Are they angels or demons?
What is the knowledge I betrayed
In choosing to be human?

Awake beside my wife, I lay.
In a minute, or an hour,
When the common light of day
Had turned her inside out again,
I would see the dark power
In her eyes, and the other men.

At the Grave of Silone

Lost in the fog at four thousand feet
When the lights come on, I can see them all,
The mountain villages, so small
A blind man feels his way about
Without a stick, and everyone overhears
Everyone else, as they quarrel and shout,
And still they are all alone —
And the places, the years,
Who redeems them? I think again
Of you, Ignazio Silone,
Ten years dead, a hundred miles to the south
On this freezing Apennine chain,
A body interred, forever looking out
On an endlessly fertile plain —

And how we had visited you, one day
When August blew the crops awake
And harvesters toiled, in the drained lake
Of human promise. . . . Skies were passing away
But nothing had changed on the ground.
Heat and apathy, everyday sound
In your natal village. Unsuccess
With its local dreamers, revving their motorbikes,
Punishing the slot machines.
Fontamara . . . it could have been
Aranyaprathet, or Ballaghaderreen.
Without knowing it, we had come to pray
At the shrine of ordinariness —
We, who were running away.

And look at us now, a man and woman
Dodging the Reaper, saving hay
In the high Abruzzo, our windowpanes
Rattled by cold, and the sonic vibrations,
Extraterrestrial, superhuman,
Of half a dozen airforce planes
That shatter the peace. . . . Again, night falls
On this village of limitations
We have come to. Invisible forces spray
Their DUCE-VINCEREMO on our walls.
As your books say,
All of us dream, and stay in thrall
To the usual consolations.
Marriage. America. Going away.

I shut the window, bank the fire,
And pick up Plato on The Good.
The lumberjack, who gives us wood
For nothing, I see him across in the bar
Where a girl is slicing lemons, tidying shelves,
And shadows argue, the porkpie hats
Of failures home from Canada, playing skat
And fourhand poker. Metal crutches,
Phlegm —the man absurdity trails
Like a village dog . . . If they saw themselves
For just one instant, as they are,
Heroic, but misunderstood,
Their conversations would carry for miles
Like the sound of a shot.

Castelli, Cerqueto, cold San Giorgio
Float in the fog, red atmospheres
Connected to each other, and to here,
Where I link your fate with hers and mine,
Unconsciousness everywhere. . . . Fifty years ago,
In exile, writing *Bread and Wine*,
The War was coming. Now, below your shrine,
Memory tries to wake
Blind monuments to the Fascist dead,
Disheartened villages, men who cannot shake
The ant of toil from their Sunday clothes,
Slatternly women, old for their years,
The Christian cross, the Communist rose,
With the human word you said.

The River

When I was angry, I went to the river —
New water on old stones, the patience of pools.
Let the will find its own pace,
Said a voice inside me
I was learning to believe,

And the rest will take care of itself.
The fish were facing upstream, tiny trout
Suspended like souls, in their aquaeous element.
I and my godlike shadow
Fell across them, and they disappeared.

All this happened deep in the mountains —
Anger, trout, and shadow
With the river flowing through them.
Far away, invisible but imagined,
Was an ancient sea, where things would resolve themselves.

In Earthquake Country

Slow as a landscape, character forms
In front of us, through a window in the mountains
Looking inwards and outwards together
At lines of nature, sandstone weathering,
Rifts that open between us, rifts that dissolve,
Except for the seams in our faces
As we grow older.

Look north, at the Apennines,
Their old faultlines. Earthquake country —
Blind tectonic plates
Are shifting the ground beneath us,
Our mediterranean floor. Forget villages
And forests of dwarf oak. Here, life
Roots itself in the inhuman.

A valley of soulmaking —
Where does it lead to? Glacial waters meet
Down there, where we cannot see them,
Roaring in our ears
All night, while we hold each other
In this cold planetarium of lights
That closes us in, the children of Galileo.

Do they see us, as we see ourselves,
The windows turning gold? Good night, dear heart,
And better luck than the dead
From Naples to Avezzano —histories, loves
Before our time, that the epicentres swallowed —
While faith that moves mountains
Tolls upvalley, in its fissured belltower.

Crossing the Apennines

In Spring, we went back to the high valleys,
You and I. Already, there were cyclamens
Huddled together for warmth, like the flames of a primus stove
On the cold forest floor. Empty woods
Awaiting leafage, drenched in April light,
A roar of mountain water
Everywhere in earshot. Electric,
Inquisitive, animals puzzled us out
For the strangers we were, with the Roman road beneath us
Cut like a groove of ageless repetition
Out of the winter. Healing mosses,
Moist green sphagnum, thickened
Like patches of living warmth, on the north face of everything.

There was always another side, but we lived on this side,
So close beneath our own particular mountain
We lost sight of it. Even now,
With the visibility clearing
On the high arêtes, there was something brooding
Out of doors, that had cooped us in seclusion
Months on end, stalled
In a wintry kitchen, icepicks hung on the wall,
A hearth of cold ashes, and trouble gathering head
In our darker selves. . . .
I would like to say
We crossed the Apennines, kept to the ancient way
As so many had done before us —
Watersheds, the invisible line
Where intuition is strengthened
And love becomes certainty. No, it was not like that.
Leached soils, yes, and the bones of cattle
At six thousand feet, where the snowline started.
And those impossibly high meadows
Where silent horses surrounded us, like trusting spirits
Expecting sugar, and we fed them salt.

Taking the Waters

There are taps that flow, all day and all night,
From the depths of Europe,
Inexhaustible, taken for granted,

Slaking our casual thirsts
At a railway station
Heading south, or here in the Abruzzo

Bursting cold from an iron standpipe
While our blind mouths
Suck at essentials, straight from the water table.

Our health is too good, we are not pilgrims,
And the nineteenth century
Led to disaster. Aix, and Baden Baden —

Where are they now, those ladies with the vapours
Sipping at glasses of hydrogen sulphide
Every morning, while the pump-house piano played

And Russian radicals steamed and stewed
For hours in their sulphur tubs
Plugged in to the cathodes of Revolution?

Real cures, for imaginary ailments —
Diocletian's, or Vespasian's.
History passes, only the waters remain,

Bubbling up, through their carbon sheets,
To the other side of catastrophe
Where we drink, at a forgotten source,

Through the old crust of Europe
Centuries deep, restored by a local merchant
Of poultry and greens, inscribing his name in Latin.

The Better Portion

The husband loved early mornings.
But the wife, give or take
The twenty percent in all of us
Open to change, slept on
To a different clock, her nightgown
A rectangle of white calico
Cut from the template of darkness.

Light changed in the various rooms
But only he saw it. . . . Afternoons
Were their common ground — the hot infusions
Brewed at four, the casual chat
As something came to the boil
Or simmered away, depending
On who was in charge, and who not,

And which year it was. Outside
Could have been anywhere, a world
Improvised, for argument's sake,
From the barking of neighbourhood dogs
Or a car backfiring, smells
And habits, the usual bottomless wells —
But this is beside the point,

As all who are paid to listen
Could have told him. . . .
                    Suddenly
One evening, she talked a blue streak
From half-past-eleven
To four-fifteen, then fell asleep
Like a stone disappearing into the deep.
All this comes from nowhere,

He told himself, flabbergasted
And unmanned, with the working surface
Of marriage all around him
To hold on to — heart and head,
The better portion neither disputed
In all their years of breaking bread
Before she emerged, from the underworld.

The Poet Sandro Penna, in Old Age

There are those who will leave this world
On a gun-carriage, draped in the flag of the state
Like my friend Montale,
Always so careful, always so astute,
So politically in the right,
With his place in the Senate, his Nobel prize
Like a state of grace
This side, at least, of eternal night —

And there are those, like my old friend
Pasolini, his bloodied head
Kicked in by a male prostitute
In Ostia — it could so easily
Have been him and me! —
Splashed all over the Roman evening papers,
Coming, in public, to scandalous ends
In the underworld of the id —

And there is me,
Sandro Penna, turned seventy
Last summer, without votes of congratulation
Or unexpurgated editions
Of the sexual poems. A fancier of boys
All my life, I have been.
For this the critics call me 'The last of the Greeks,
The most ancient of men. . . .'

Ernesto, Quintilio, beloved Raffaele —
A cigarette or an ice-cream
Could buy your caresses, outside the Termini Station.
To the conviction of your beauty I held fast
When the tortured screams
From Gestapo headquarters rang in our ears
Through the endless months of the German occupation.
Did you only recognise me
By my bitten nails, like all pederasts?*

Nembutal, Mogadon, Tavar, and Mictasol
Turning my urine blue —
I am old, alone. My reputation? It's invisible —
A poet, they say, for the very few
Who see, through the mists of the twentieth century,
The universal, the sun coming through.
To the journalists
I can only say, not even trying to make sense,
'My past is risible. . . .'

Søren Kierkegaard

I took you north with me, Kierkegaard,
Always intending to read you. On the train
I had nine straight hours, from Florence through to Munich
In a closed compartment. . . . Marshalling yards
At Bologna, the north Italian plain

That seemed to stretch forever — apples, wine,
The childhood of humanity, acres of vines
And orchards blossoming with original sin
Through windows looking outwards, looking in.
I never got down to it, your grand design —

*Roman street lore, 1930s.

The Stages on Life's Way were watersheds
I stretched my legs at, took the air
At fabulous, but earthly, altitudes,
Where Austrians boarded, girls with golden hair.
Serious, bookish, riding the corridors

Into Germany, scions of adult races,
These are your readership, Kierkegaard.
The ethical life, the Protestant rage
At ecstasy, bought at a station —
I never got beyond the opening page. . . .

Kierkegaard, I can see you shake your head
In disappointment at the sons of men
From everywhere north of the Alps, a land of the dead
Your spirit inhabits, ghosting your own books —
The Sickness Unto Death. The Concept of Dread.

Bavarian traffic streams through the needle's eye
Of a manmade tunnel. Almost done
Our northward journey, and the autobahn
Keeps pace with us, converging
On Munich. . . . What would you know of joy,

Kierkegaard, you who hated poets,
Or the million things that pass through one man's mind
In nine hours' transit, all the way through from Florence,
Feeding his soul on headphones,
Dreaming of women. Things you would not understand.

Night Train through the Brenner

Why should it seem so strange
To be travelling backwards
Out of Germany, as the hours change,

With the whole of history
In reverse, the passengers sleeping
On fettered wheels, and everyone in the dark?

When we left, it was after midnight.
New Year rockets fizzling out
On the Munich streets — a litter of celebration,

Firecrackers, broken glass,
And two hundred years of revolution
Lingering, like a sulphur smell in the nostrils. . . .

The conductor coughs in the corridor
All night long. He can have our identities
If he gives them back in the morning

Rubberstamped. Our one desire
Is to sleep in the peace
Of body heat — let no torch shine among us! —

While someone else deciphers
The moving lights from their reflections,
The true direction of time. . . .

The Alps are not our business —
Innsbrück, Brenner, Bolzano. A roar in our ears
As we bore through tunnels —

The watersheds of Europe
Were always too cold for us. Better to dream
Of Munich with its Christmas lights

Or the mannequins of Florence,
At one of which we will certainly wake
The morning after the ages.

Towards daybreak, the sound of voices —
An unknown station. How long have we been here?
An hour? A night? Two hundred years?

Italian speech, on a megaphone
'... *Bologna, Firenze, binario tre* ...'
Drifts through the darkness. Been and gone

Is Nineteen Hundred and Eighty Nine —
The heights are behind us. Early vendors
Push their steaming trolleys

Through the small hours of Day One.
Two tramps, a railwayman,
In the light of a station buffet,

Swallow their bitter portion. For an instant
Life is the same for all of us,
Bleary-eyed, at the dawn of humanity.

The Canto of Ulysses

As the eye reads, from left to right,
Ulysses' canto, what comes next,
The day, already spread like a text
On the ceiling above me, asks to be read.
Anxiety, or increasing light,
Whatever wakes me, fills my head
With the oceanic billows
Of a slept-in marriage bed.

The shutters go up, like thunder,
On the street below. If the soul fed
On coffee, aromatic bread,
Niceties raised to the power of art,
We would long ago have knuckled under
To perfection, in the green heart
Of Italy, settled here,
And gone to sleep in the years.

But what was it Dante said
About ordinary life? My mind wanders
Like Ulysses, through the early sounds,
A motor starting, taps turned on,
Unravelling Penelope's skein,
Unsatisfied, for the millionth time,
With merely keeping my feet on the ground —
As if I could ever go home!

Money, like a terrible shadow,
Unsuccess, and middle age,
Darken my vision of the page
I scan from memory, where it says
Women will all be widows
To the quest, neglected fathers,
Ageing, live out lonely days,
And coastlines merge with each other.

Sound of a passing train at dawn
Through Umbrian fields, of wheat and vines,
Through cloisters and bird sanctuaries,
Feeding on overhead powerlines,
Obsesses me, like the need to be gone,
Vitality, or cowardice,
The sail of Ulysses, west of the sun,
Dwindling in ptolemaic skies.

What did you say to me last night?
'Where you go, I go.' Sleep on that
While I watch you, curled,
Uxorious, my one satisfaction
At the heart of the known world,
Stippled with mediterranean light,
Its yellow streaks already latent
With afternoon heat, and stupefaction.

Any day now, we hand back the key
To habit, peace, stability,
The seasonal round, festivities
Of wine and cherry. Think of the fuss
Of what to take, and leave behind —
Shade for the soul, our miniature trees
Of olive, oak, and southern pine —
Before the seas close over us.

Reductio

I could spend the rest of my life
simply drawing a table and two chairs.
—Alberto Giacometti

What is big? What is extended in space?
Not this studio surely, not this glass
On a wooden table, or the apple
Trapped forever in the intersecting planes
Of redemptive vision. Certainly not this face—
But the rue d'Alésia, outside in the rain,
The millions of strange people
Whirled like atoms through the hub of Montparnasse

As night comes down, and the lit conceptual cages,
Dome, Select, Rotonde, the stamping-grounds
Of seeing and being seen, the gilt cafés
And mirrored brothels of the rue de l'Echaudé,
Where goddesses file naked on the stage,
Invite appraisal, and your mind's hot foundry
Casts them in bronze, remote as steles,
Cycladic or Sumerian, ancestral but still real.

What is big? What is extended in space?
Not the little tin soldiers, oh so small
In toyshop windows, though they say it all.
Not the yellow decals, not the pedestrian lights,
Stationary Man or Walking Man, in the night's
Electric statuary. Not the living gaze
Forever fugitive, but only the skull,
The pleasure-seekers after hours, crashed out

On benches and late metros, heads agape
In a staring void. 'All the living are dead'
It suddenly hits you. No, not Woman now, not Tree —
And where did it get you, that theft of bread
In childhood? Not Paris now, but infinities
Of disconnected people, faces, times,
Humanity dissolving into shapes
At the ends of avenues, at the ends of rhymes.

What is big now? What is extended in space?
A single tungsten bulb, a Palace-at-Four,
Your lean-to shed. Inside it, memory swarms
With ancient heads, in the depths of revolving doors
Beheld, forgotten . . . From table to wooden chair
Saharas spread. A glass suspended in air —
You take a drink. To keep your fingers warm
You busy yourself, with the one loved face
Attempted endlessly, with the one loved form.

Bare Arm

When the blind goes up
In the morning, one bare arm,
A woman's, from the dormer
Opposite, swims up

To the surface of her life
And turns away,
A mother, a housewife,
To the depths of her own day —

And the skies flow past,
And the silvered glass
Reflects them, her window
No one can see into,

Except, one night
Of sultry weather,
Energies, stray lightnings,
We glimpsed each other

Naked, in the small hours,
Coming from showers
And lovemaking, two spouses
In opposite houses

Pausing, in the lit frame
Of revelation,
Not knowing each other's name,
Uncaring, unconditional

For once, two creatures
Awake, while everyone slept,
Alive in the forest
Of second nature.

Reading Saint Augustine

Huge stanzas, on the end of the world,
Were crowding in like weather, scudding cloud
And changing light, on Monday the twenty-third
At the breakfast table. Light of heart
And casual, with the working week ahead,
We went to our rooms. Again, the traffic noise
Outside my window. Quieter, outside yours,
A garden, finches, at the back of the house.
And this we called our discipline, our art,
Internal, focussed, warding off the powers
Of dissolution, each in our own small way,
Ideal or real, sufficing unto the day.

As for myself, I was desperate to get back
Behind Augustine's *City of God*
To a time before our time, of plunder and sack,
Where the word Apocalypse was clearly stated.
Better not to write then, just to read —
To read and listen, only to bring in later
Everyday life, the baker up at four
Around the corner, six months from retirement
And his millionth loaf, the silence of mid-morning
On every floor, the boy delivering fliers,
The postgirl with her sad impetigoed face,
When the Beginning and End were definitely in place.

As for you, I hesitate to speak —
Doing it better that I, whatever you did —
With your pregnant myth, expanding by the hour,
Incorporating gardens into the Garden,
Burrowing into consciousness and id,
Abandoning Logos, cultivating Psyche,
Plot and character, what the butler saw
Of more than manners — in a word, real life,
For what did anyone know of Eternal Law?
Bypassing the Sublime for someone's grief,
Irrational, undignified, humanly true,
Staying faithful only to what you knew.

Eleven thirty. Carthage and Thagaste
Long since fallen, knew their gods had failed.
Alaric and his Huns had stove them in
Like Rome before them. Adeodatus the bastard
Of Augustine, and Augustine himself, were dead.
All that was left, now, was the *City of God*.
The orgies, the pomaded boys, the love-ins,
All were over. Outside, sirens wailed —
A truck rolled by, the windowglass vibrated.
Otherwise, all was normal. In your room
Another sentence formed. *For even without him*
Her life would go on. I stood in the kitchen, waited

For coffee to boil, and time to come to an end.
Monday, the day for maids. Behind the garden
Whiteclad women put their house in order.
One, who had just stayed over, ran her hands
Along her cheekbones, loving herself in a mirror,
Rubbing facecream in. A morning after —
Sinless, without guilt. Supernatural terror?
I could hear her hard, ironical laughter
Echoing through the ages, the sacked empires,
Back to Alaric. No, on the twenty-third,
For all its cloud-apocalypse funeral pyres,
Women, it seemed, would have the final word.

The Daughters of Lot

They were born, the daughters of Lot,
Facing the wrong direction.
A cart was loaded, a donkey stolen —
Now they cling to their Father,
Not looking back. Behind them
The site of disaster,
Immemorial. Meteor-showers
Bloom like rockets, magnesium flares
In an underlit sky. Benighted
The city burns, its merchant houses —
Buy if there's a run, but otherwise wait —
Settling, like silt, in the dregs of a harbour
Clogged with shipwrecks, while the fleet,
Offshore, of the new administrators,
Stays for surrender.
  There they go,
The pair of them, and the one man in their life,
Through a hole blown in the cliff
Called Mother, her salt profile
Staring backwards, into the time before birth —
Baby, I never loved you. Make my day
And pack your bags. . . . — a hole big enough
For a motorway, if there were still petrol,
And cars were for more than sleeping in,
And speeds outran the Bible.

They have eyes, now, for the present only.
Baccanalia reigns. Smashed amphorae,
Scattered rations. Drunks beneath the jesse tree
On the last of their own good wine.
The founding of houses, the birth of children —
Now, it will never happen.
Their father, instead, is their husband.
Sodomites and sodomised,
They are breaking bread together.

Dennis O'Driscoll

Someone

someone is dressing up for death today, a change of skirt or tie
eating a final feast of buttered sliced pan, tea
scarcely having noticed the erection that was his last
shaving his face to marble for the icy laying out
spraying with deodorant her coarse armpit grass
someone today is leaving home on business
saluting, terminally, the neighbours who will join in the cortege
someone is paring his nails for the last time, a precious moment
someone's waist will not be marked with elastic in the future
someone is putting out milkbottles for a day that will not come
someone's fresh breath is about to be taken clean away
someone is writing a cheque that will be rejected as 'drawer deceased'
someone is circling posthumous dates on a calendar
someone is listening to an irrelevant weather forecast
someone is making rash promises to friends
someone's coffin is being sanded, laminated, shined
who feels this morning quite as well as ever
someone if asked would find nothing remarkable in today's date
perfume and goodbyes her final will and testament
someone today is seeing the world for the last time
as innocently as he had seen it first

Stillborn

What we are lamenting
Is what has not been
And what will not have seen
This mild May morning.

What we are lamenting
Is unsuckled air
And what was brought to bear
This mild May morning.

What we are lamenting
Is our flesh and blood, this child
That has not laughed or cried
This mild May morning.

What we are lamenting
Is the life we crave
Snatched from the cradle to the grave
This mild May morning.

Conception

scum of humanity
seed of pain

multiple warheads
arms racing to stake their claim

the triumphant achieve spina bifida
or ambition malnutrition or fame

and hundreds of millions of sprigs
are disseminated in vain

a lost civilisation
a bedclothes stain

Spoiled Child

my child recedes inside me
and need never puzzle where it came from
or lose a football in the dusty laurel bushes
or sneak change from my jacket to buy sweets

my child will not engage in active military service
or make excuses about its school report
or look up from a picture book, dribbling a pink smile
or qualify for free glasses or school lunch

my child will not become a prodigy of musicianship or crime
and will evince no appetite for hamburgers or drugs
and will suffer neither orgasm nor kidney stones
reduced neither to a statistic nor a sacrifice

my child will not play space games with its cousins
or sit adrift on a grandparent's choppy lap
or slit its wrists or erect a loving headstone on my grave
or store a secret name for frogs or treetops

my child will not be a comfort to my old age
my child will not be cheated or promoted or denied
my child will trail me, like a guardian angel, all my life
its blemishes, its beauty, its shortcomings and promise

forever unsullied and unfulfilled

Fruit Salad

I. PEACH

There's not much point in trying
to cultivate a sultry peach of words.
Just pass me one to stroke, to eat,
or paint it from a glowing palette;
colours dart from apricot to apple,
flames licking velvet hide.
Hold its downy, yielding roundness,
fondle its lightly clothed contours,
taste its golden mean, its sweetness,
before it starts to shrink and shrivel,
starts to wrinkle like a passion fruit.

II. STRAWBERRY

Strawberries with whipped cream,
a sunset ripple on your plate...
A cordate locket, a precious stone;
cut one and expose the marbled core.
The wholesome rubicundity of outdoors,
not the hothouse plastic of tomatoes;
compact, meaty, flecked with seeds,
the bracts a garnish (parsley on beef,
verdant ferns in a bouquet of roses).
A July day provides the ideal accompaniment,
lazy as the cream dripping from the whisk.

III. PEAR

Most easily hurt of fruits,
bruising under a matt coat of skin,
smooth as bath soap inside;
halved, a perfectly stringed lute.
It hangs in a shaft of autumn light
timeless as a bronze cathedral bell
or disturbs the peace and drops
— a hand grenade, pin still intact,
a toppling shell of glycerine.
We take refuge from our troubles in its syrup,
wasps burrowing through heady pulp.

IV. APPLE

All apples lead back to that first temptation:
trees behind the thatched farmhouse,
forbidden fruit, a warts-and-all beauty,
pupating in pink silk blossom
then fired and glazed in summer,
brushed by a red admiral's wings,
wine-dipped like nectarines or green
as nettles stinging with tart knowledge.
Bite the way back to a primal silence,
your rhythmic crunch shutting out
the world, digesting its hard truths.

V. FRUIT SHOP

Orange skins baked to a crust
(fluffy whiteness underneath);
raspberries like bleeding gums;
melons whose haunches
are tested for ripeness . . .
I buy bananas racked like chops
and apricots, one blemished
with a spot (which I'll slice off,
cheddar flesh wholesome again).
I pinch a bulbous, plum-size grape.
Lemons tumble from an opened crate.

Residuary Estates

I.

After the nausea
of chemotherapy,
after the vomit
and the sores,
bald patients rest
on pillows stuffed
with long hair
from Treblinka,
sleep off
the side-effects
of God and man.

II.

Cancerous cells are immortal
laboratory tests suggest.

Is this the everlasting life
my mother now enjoys

that she had prayed for:
the life beyond the grave?

III. *After Bertolt Brecht*

wasted by illness
left for dead

flowers rooted
in her soiled body

to weigh so little
she must have taken

enormous pains

IV.

the calm between storms
is the silence in which
the dead are not named
until relatives are informed

Misunderstanding and Muzak

You are in the Super Valu supermarket
expecting to meet me at 6.15.

I am in the Extra Valu supermarket
expecting to meet you at 6.15.

Danny Boy is calling you down special-offer aisles.
Johann Strauss is waltzing me down special-offer aisles.

I weigh mushrooms and broccoli and beans.
You weigh beans and mushrooms and broccoli.

It is 6.45. No sign of you.
It is 6.45. No sign of me.

You may have had a puncture.
I may have been held up at work.

It is 6.55. You may have been murdered.
It is 6.55. I may have been flattened by a truck.

Danny Boy starts crooning all over you again.
Johann Strauss starts dancing all over me again.

Everything that's needed for our Sunday lunch
is heaped up in my trolley, your trolley.

We hope to meet somewhere, to eat it.

Reading Primo Levi on the Train

We breach the ordered peace
of our atrocity-free mornings
forsaking the solitary confinement of sleep
for transportation by commuter train
to where labour pays debts owed
to building society and bank.

We bear food parcels
— salad rolls and fruit —
our working lunches.
A woman cradles a package
— slop bucket or lampshade?
Hair clings to our heads still.
Chains hang from slender necks.
So many of us to kick, to kill,
so much flesh to torture and despise
beneath the modish cuts
of suit and skirt, so many tales
to force abruptly to an end,
so many souls expected home at dusk
to spirit away in cattle trucks . . .

The train clatters on.
Whatever this day holds
we will live to see it through,
march back down gravel drives,
their cindered, osteal sounds,
watch stars like gold-filled teeth
chatter with us in the cold.

from *The Bottom Line*

A life of small disappointments, hardly meriting
asperity or rage, an e-mail cc-ed
to the wrong address, an engagement
missed, a client presentation failing
to persuade: nothing you can't sweat off
at gym or squash. But, in the dark filling
of the night, doubts gather with the rain
which, spreading as predicted from the west,
now leaves its mark on fuscous window panes;
and you wait for apprehensions to dissolve
in the first glimmer of curtain light.

❖

Pressing tanned flesh, reaching consensus
over some outstanding fact, our well-
scrubbed, nail-filed hands feel soft.
Enough contact with the soil is made
weeding invasive seedlings from the lawn . . .
Best of all, undo the crested tie,
change into fawn slacks and turtle-neck,
white-fringed golfing shoes, commune
with nature between fairway and rough,
taking the air on a bracing Saturday
or sharing honours for the captain's prize.

❖

When you unclasp your slimline briefcase,
the apple, deep green, high gloss
with waxen sheen, a tea-break snack,
glows among the acetate reports,
symbolising something you can't name
but crave for when your sales, morale
are low —peace, a meaningful existence . . .
You settle for a rental in the west,
family away-days, the company car,
and, who can tell, later you may rise
to a weekend cottage, hens, a bright-red door.

❖

At the visitors' car park, the belts
of our trench coats flap with the wind;
we huddle in a confidential group
hoping to have pressed home the point,
a hollow Coke can tinkling on the street.
Then, despite this meeting of minds,
for one long second we run out of things
to say, permit thoughts chill as downturns
to stray into our heads until we contrive
the next move, check watch or schedule,
arrange matters arising, part on a jocose note.

❖

On the mobile to a client, or passing word
across a dealing room's array of desks,
the way you speak does not brook
disagreement — a patois of mutters and twangs.
Adjusting to home, tense still from
breasting the dense atmosphere of work,
it takes so little to set off a row.
One misplaced phrase and the avalanche
begins: a hail shower of rocks, ropes
failing to grip, your wife as an
ice-maiden throwing glacial looks.

❖

The peace of Friday evenings after
staff have left the open-plan deserted,
before cleaners key-in for their shift.
Sun flakes out on the carpet, rays
highlight staplers, calculators, pens;
phones flop in cradles: Monday will
inaugurate another week, small talk
over instant coffee; new debenture stock . . .
Meanwhile, suspended between worlds,
I drum on the plastic in-tray, stare down
at the frenzied city, disinclined to budge.

❖

How much longer will this crystal water
flow, this snow come decked in white,
I wonder, as I pour out bottled spring,
brace myself for questions from the floor
about our new cost-cutting scheme . . .
Even when I mouth defences of our safety
record —latest filters, monitors in place —
I see my children's scornful faces, rivers
shimmering like metal, aluminium-clear,
quivering with farmed fish, squirming with algae,
grey snow lodging on eroded banks . . .

❖

Can a year really have passed since our
last Christmas shindig? Here I am
in the same rut, not a single resolution
carried through, deluding myself that
I'm still in my prime. Yes, it's that
time again: a factitious peace, a ceasefire
between camps, an ambience as sweet
as fake rot on marzipan fruits doled out
from desk to desk; tomorrow's gossip will
concern the boss who'll traipse in late,
suit crumpled, manner untypically mute.

❖

The unoriginal sins we perpetrate, our guilt
shared like a Christmas bonus: mileage rigged,
spare parts purloined, an office laptop
commandeered to conserve sports club cash,
things troubling when the internal audit
section dreams up dodgy questions;
taxmen, too, the nightmare of close scrutiny
— receipts, excuses, bank statements
to prepare —and the attendant dread
of lay-offs, sackings, three-day weeks,
gaunt, haunting figures begging change.

❖

Then the time comes when you know
none of your promise will be fulfilled;
the saving roles luck, fame, deliverance
from your job were meant to play . . .
You will slave on till pension day,
eluded by advancement, satisfaction, wealth.
In your head, some plangent melody repeats;
in your mind's eye, a preview of your part
as walk-on stoic, accepting failure in good
heart, battling home against the wind
this night the same as the last.

❖

The white-cuffed sales rep, guarding
territory, does not add up in the age
of central warehousing; the few we still
keep on are doomed: jaunty, over-groomed men,
sharing jokes and samples at the check-outs,
waiting for a brisk assistant manager
to deign to acknowledge their existence,
counting pallets in a draughty store-room,
raising special offers to eye-level shelves.
Commission in decline, their smiles grow
thin; redundancy will come as no surprise.

❖

Death, once brushed against,
does not seem in the least
like a stubbly ghost with scythe
reaping dry grass in the graveyard,
but shows up as a brash executive
cutting recklessly across your lane,
lights making eye-contact with yours,
ready to meet head-on as though
by previous appointment; ram home
your car horn like a panic button:
his cellphone's bell will toll for you.

❖

Out on the open road — sun visor, shades,
a guiding hand, the reassuring buoyancy
of tyres; blues and big-band tapes plug gaps
between troubleshooting client operations.
Everywhere seems miles from everywhere,
conflated landscapes scale the heights,
as I check with my secretary by phone
that no shit has hit the HQ fan.
The man at the factory entrance-hut
directs me to the guest zone; I lean
back, grab my linen jacket from its hook.

❖

Scarcely to be acknowledged, even to myself,
days when the very sight of my wall planner
makes me sick, when — instead of tough,
decisive judgements delivered with a quick
peremptory scrawl — I sculpt a paper clip,
chew a ballpoint, gaze at the Alpine calendar.
Suit-coat removed, I scroll through e-mail;
there are press releases to issue, markets
to nail . . . I must switch back to fast track,
delegate; late again tonight, home to my
sleeping child, a wife's taciturn rebuke.

❖

Over decades, I have said goodbye
to my retiring colleagues, signed
the sentimental cards slyly passed
around, tossed notes into collection
envelopes, stared at grey down fringing
a hand that squeezes mine, conveying
as much emotion as it dares betray . . .
We promise to stay in touch but, of
course, we never do after the hearty
speeches end (tributes, in-jokes from
friends) and they drop out of our cast.

❖

Walking through the automatic exit,
talking heatedly about the downside
of a greenfield site, I am captivated
by a busker's tune: untainted, pure,
drawn from the rainswept mountainy mind
of an old man counting yearlings in the wind,
the log-shifting silence of his hearth . . .
That music keeps its nerve, unfazed
by the pressing business of the streets;
you continue — 'Right?', 'OK?'— but I,
thread lost, can only mumble and concur.

❖

The flimsiness of steep buildings,
scintillant ice palaces of glass;
sun-spots, structures opposite are
mirrored, warped; filing cabinets,
work stations, rubber plants in tubs
prove amenable to public scrutiny.
It is like walking on air, the sheer
vertiginous layers of stacked light;
lifts surge through molten floors
or plunge to solidities of sculpted bronze,
revolving doors, terrazzo, guards.

❖

A monumentally awful day, shopfloor staff
baying for your blood; sighs, grumbles,
union officials clamouring for redress . . .
Then the recriminations taking you aback:
like a drowning life, your past is
brandished on the far side of the desk,
your certainty about the fairness
of the way you run the branch is challenged,
old feuds reopen and, with tension high,
you still maintain control, adopt a mild,
sincere tone, just as the books advise.

❖

Not afraid of risks, not listening to
cagey advice; striking out from time
to time, irrespective of whose toes
you're forced to tread on — whatever's
needed to bring your plans on-stream.
However tight the ship, there will always
be some weak links in line management:
bypass them, oblige the shirkers
to shape up or go — any fallout from your
hardline approach may be made good in
due course; meanwhile, stand your ground.

❖

You could do it in your sleep, the dawn
trek through another empty terminal,
vinyl undergoing a mechanical shine,
gift shops shut — cigars, frilled silk
behind steel grilles —bales of early
papers bursting to blurt out their news . . .
Fanning stale air with your boarding pass,
if you look up from your business-class recliner
during the safety drill, it will be only
to eyeball the stewardess; you itch
to switch your laptop on, rejig the unit price.

❖

Some networking is necessary to get
to the right people, turning on the charm,
having them eat out of your palm, but never
put entirely on the spot, everything off
the record, a once-only concession you
won't mention to your friends, strictly
between yourselves, without prejudice . . .
Futile dealing with less senior staff,
sticklers for detail, holding progress back.
At clubs, committees, conferences, make a point
of banging heads together, picking brains.

❖

Sensor lights tested, alarm code set,
I burrow into the high-tog, duckdown duvet;
the number-crunching radio-clock squanders
digital minutes like there was no tomorrow.
Who will remember my achievements when
age censors me from headed notepaper?
Sometimes, if I try to pray, it is with
dead colleagues that I find myself communing . . .
At the end of the day, for my successors too,
what will cost sleep are market forces, vagaries
of share price, p/e ratio, the bottom line.

Water

The miracle of water
is that it tastes of nothing,
neither of chlorine nor peat,
not of old tap fittings or dead sheep.

Water was the first mirror,
drinking images of beauty,
showing their wrinkled future
in the mildest breeze.

Water clings to its neutrality,
changes state at boiling point,
finds the level at which
tensions cool, limbs relax.

It is the splinter of ice in the heart,
the white blood of the snowman,
the burst main flooding
from Christ's frozen side.

Them and You

They wait for the bus.
You spray them with puddles.

They queue for curry and chips.
You phone an order for delivery.

They place themselves under the protection
of the Marian Grotto at the front of their estate.

You put your trust in gilts, managed funds,
income continuation plans.

They look weathered.
You look tanned.

They knock back pints.
You cultivate a taste for vintage wines.

They get drunk.
You get pleasantly inebriated.

Their wives have straw hair.
Yours is blonde.

They are missing one football card
to complete the full set.

You keep an eye out for a matching
Louis XV-style walnut hall table.

They are hoping for a start with a builder.
You play your part in the family firm.

They use loose change, welfare coupons.
You tap your credit card impatiently on the counter.

They lean over the breeze-block wall to gossip.
You put down motions for the Residents' AGM.

They have a hot tip for Newmarket.
You have the inside track on a rights issue.

They go over the top.
You reach it.

They preach better pay.
You practise it.

Either

They are somewhere in the world, pouring soya milk
on porridge during the dream-time before work,
        or sprouting thick fungal whiskers
        in a graveyard's penetrating damp —
the ones I used to know, with whom I lost
touch, who were once the mainstay of my
        gossip: squash partners, office colleagues,
        obnoxious neighbours, friends of friends.

As I speak, they scrutinise the milk carton's text
or subside more comfortably into the sleep
        that resurrection's long-haul wait entails.
        Our paths crossed, then grassed over again.
They are either alive and well or decomposing
slowly in a shroud; I could either call them up
        and chat, or confirm that they are ex-directory now.
        It is a matter of life or death.

Nor

'There didn't have to be 2,000 diseases
of the skin', I remember someone commenting.
Nor 17,293 painfully slow routes through the vomitory
before being thrown to the lions of death.
Nor 11,416 ways of feeling wounded.
Nor 89,010 gradations of loneliness
calibrated on traffic islands, country lanes.
Nor 29,109,352 reasons to toss and turn at night.
Nor stage fright, nor honeymoon cystitis.
Nor *esprit de l'escalier*, nor so many calories in cream.
Nor sexually transmitted fatalities, nor smoker's cough.
Nor 250,000,000 tons (live weight) of humanity
to experience these things, nor however many
newborn pounds were dragged screaming, added
to the tally, since my opening line.

In Memory of Alois Alzheimer
(1864–1915)

I.

Before this page fades from memory,
spare a thought for Alois Alzheimer,
called to mind each time

someone becomes forgetful,
disintegration vindicating
his good name.

II.

His is the last image assigned
to the ex-President who has slipped
from public view; soiled sheets
give credence to his thesis;

his territory is marked out
by the track of urine
dribbled along the corridor
of the day-care centre.

III.

Lie closer to me in the dry sheets
while I can still tell who you are.

Let me declare how much I love you
before our bed is sorely tested.

Love me with drooling toxins, with carbon monoxide,
with rope, with arrows through my heart.

Tomorrow

I.

Tomorrow I will start to be happy.
The morning will light up like a celebratory cigar.
Sunbeams sprawling on the lawn will set
dew sparkling like a cut-glass tumbler of champagne.
Today will end the worst phase of my life.

I will put my shapeless days behind me,
fencing off the past, as a golden rind
of sand parts slipshod sea from solid land.
It is tomorrow I want to look back on, not today.
Tomorrow I start to be happy; today is almost yesterday.

II.

Australia, how wise you are to get the day
over and done with first, out of the way.
You have eaten the fruit of knowledge, while
we are dithering about which main course to choose.
How liberated you must feel, how free from doubt:

the rise and fall of stocks, today's closing prices
are revealed to you before our speculating has begun.
Australia, you can gather in your accident statistics
like a harvest while our roads still have hours to kill.
When we are in the dark, you have sagely seen the light.

III.

Cagily, presumptuously, I dare to write 2018.
A date without character or tone. 2018.
A year without interest rates or mean daily temperature.
Its hit songs have yet to be written, its new-year
babies yet to be induced, its truces to be signed.

Much too far off for prophecy, though one hazards
a tentative guess — a so-so year most likely,
vague in retrospect, fizzling out with the usual
end-of-season sales; everything slashed:
your last chance to salvage something of its style.

Towards a Cesare Pavese Title

(Verrà la Morte e Avrà i Tuoi Occhi)

Death will come and it will wear your eyes.

Death demands the handover of your eyes.

Death eyes you, stares you in the face.

Then death assumes the running of your eyes.

Death powders cheeks, shadows eyes.

Death would take the eyes out of your head.

Death will seize your assets, cut off your eye supply.

Death lashes out at your defenceless eyes.

You are up to your eyes in death.

Death takes after you, eyes the image of yours.

You would recognise death with your eyes shut.

Death will give you dagger glances, evil eyes.

Death makes eye contact at last.

Death will come and it will steal your looks.

Weather Permitting

I.

The August day you wake to takes you by surprise.
Its bitterness. Black sullen clouds. Brackish downpour.
A drift-net of wetness enmeshes the rented cottage,
towels and children's swimwear sodden on the line.

Dry-gulleted drains gulp down neat rain.
Drops bounce from a leaking gutter with hard,
uncompromising slaps: and, like resignation
in the face of death, you contemplate winter

with something close to tenderness, the sprint
from fuel shed to back door, the leisurely
ascent of peat smoke, even the suburban haze
of boiler flues when thermostats are set.

You warm to those thoughts as you sit there,
brainstorming ways to keep the family amused,
plans abandoned for barefoot games on dry sand.
Handcraft shops? Slot-machine arcades? Hotel grills?

In truth —manipulating toast crumbs backwards,
forwards at the unsteady table's edge —you'd prefer
to return to your bed as if with some mild
ailment, pampered by duvet, whiskey, cloves.

II.

Let it rain.
Let the clouds discharge their contents like reserve tanks.
Let the worms burrow their way to the topsoil
from whatever dank Sargasso they were spawned in.
Let dampness rot the coffin-boards of the summer house.
Let the shrubs lose their foothold in the wind,
the nettles lose their edge, the drenched rat
with slicked-back hair scuttle to its sewage pipe.
Let the tropical expanses of the rhubarb leaves
serve as an artificial pond, a reservoir.
Let the downpour's impact on the toolshed be akin
to the dull applause on an archive recording of a love duet.
Let the bricklayers at the building site wrap
pathetic sheets of polythene around doomed foundations.
Let the limb ripped from the tree's socket
hover fleetingly in the air, an olive branch.
Let a rainbow's fantail unfurl like a bird of paradise.
Let a covenant be sealed, its wording watertight.
Let the floods recede.
Let there be light.

III. *After Giacomo Leopardi*

The storm runs out of wind; nature, which
abhors a silence, fills the vacancy with birdsong.
Deserting the airless, low-ceilinged coop,
the hen repeats herself ad infinitum. Replenished
like the rain-barrels, hearts grow sanguine.

Hammering resumes. Humming. Gossip. Croons.
Sun strides down lanes that grass has repossessed,
takes a shine to the brasses at the hotel where,
by the window she thrust open, the chambermaid
is marvelling at the cleansed freshness, calm.

Balm of mind and body. Will we ever feel
more reconciled to life than now, ever
know a moment more conducive to new hopes,
eager beginnings, auspicious starts?
How easily pleased we are. Rescind

the threat of torment for the briefest
second and we blot out dark nights of the soul
when lightning flashes fanned by wind
ignited fire and brimstone visions.
Sorrow is perennial; happiness, a rare

bloom, perfumes the air —so that we breathe
with the ease of a camphor-scented chest
from which congestion has just lifted.
Lack of woe equates with rapture then,
though not till death will pain take full leave

of our senses, grant us permanent relief.

Nocturne

Time for sleep. Time for a nightcap of grave music,
a dark nocturne, a late quartet, a parting song,
bequeathed by the great dead in perpetuity.

I catch a glance sometimes of my own dead at the window,
those whose traits I share: thin as moths, as matchsticks,
they stare into the haven of the warm room, eyes ablaze.

It is Sunday a lifetime ago. A woman in a now-demolished house
sings *Michael, Row the Boat Ashore* as she sets down the bucket
with its smooth folds of drinking water . . .

The steadfast harvest moon out there, entangled in the willow's
stringy hair, directs me home like T'ao Ch'ien: *A caged bird*
pines for its first forest, a salmon thirsts for its stream.

Missing God

His grace is no longer called for
before meals: farmed fish multiply
without His intercession.
Bread production rises through
disease-resistant grains devised
scientifically to mitigate His faults.

Yet, though we rebelled against Him
like adolescents, uplifted to see
an oppressive father banished —
a bearded hermit — to the desert,
we confess to missing Him at times.

Miss Him during the civil wedding
when, at the blossomy altar
of the registrar's desk, we wait in vain
to be fed a line containing words
like 'everlasting' and 'divine'.

Miss Him when the TV scientist
explains the cosmos through equations,
leaving our planet to revolve on its axis
aimlessly, a wheel skidding in snow.

Miss Him when the radio catches a snatch
of plainchant from some echoey priory;
when the gospel choir raises its collective voice
to ask *Shall We Gather at the River?*
or the forces of the oratorio converge
on *I Know That My Redeemer Liveth*
and our contracted hearts lose a beat.

Miss Him when a choked voice at
the crematorium recites the poem
about fearing no more the heat of the sun.

Miss Him when we stand in judgement
on a lank Crucifixion in an art museum,
its stripe-like ribs testifying to rank.

Miss Him when the gamma-rays
recorded on the satellite graph
seem arranged into a celestial score,
the music of the spheres,
the *Ave Verum Corpus* of the observatory lab.

Miss Him when we stumble on the breast lump
for the first time and an involuntary prayer
escapes our lips; when a shadow crosses
our bodies on an x-ray screen; when we receive
a transfusion of foaming blood
sacrificed anonymously to save life.

Miss Him when we exclaim His name
spontaneously in awe or anger
as a woman in a birth ward
calls to her long-dead mother.

Miss Him when the linen-covered
dining table holds warm bread rolls,
shiny glasses of red wine.

Miss Him when a dove swoops
from the orange grove in a tourist village
just as the monastery bell begins to take its toll.

Miss Him when our journey leads us
under leaves of Gothic tracery, an arch
of overlapping branches that meet
like hands in Michelangelo's *Creation.*

Miss Him when, trudging past a church,
we catch a residual blast of incense,
a perfume on par with the fresh-baked loaf
which Milosz compared to happiness.

Miss Him when our newly-fitted kitchen
comes in Shaker-style and we order
a matching set of Mother Ann Lee chairs.

Miss Him when we listen to the prophecy
of astronomers that the visible galaxies
will recede as the universe expands.

Miss Him when the sunset makes
its presence felt in the stained glass
window of the fake antique lounge bar.

Miss Him the way an uncoupled glider
riding the evening thermals misses its tug.

Miss Him, as the lovers shrugging
shoulders outside the cheap hotel
ponder what their next move should be.

Even feel nostalgic, odd days,
for His Second Coming,
like standing in the brick
dome of a dovecote
after the birds have flown.

Full Flight

Arms outstretched,
sunbather on an inflated bed,

the overhead jet
is just that interval

from take-off at which
the stewardess announces

We shall shortly be commencing
our in-flight cabin service.

It might equally be
a speeded-up version

of Bede's fable:
a mechanical sparrow

hightailing it above
that transient banquet hall.

Thrush and Anti-Thrush

Definitely not, in the thrush's case,
a matter of fine feathers making
fine birds; yet its speckles lure the eye.
Jumpy also, a tad insecure,
walking with a sack-race hop,
legs propped at an awkward angle
like a dodgy bracket on a home-built shelf.

The brown wings and crown
are its least attractive features
by a fairly long shot,
bringing to mind musty smells
and past their sell-by-date
mushrooms, festering brain-dead
in the vegetable drawer.

Marks should be deducted too
(purely on lapse-of-taste grounds)
for its liposuction diet of flabby snails;
insects picked like scabs from walls;
rubber-band worms coiled round its snout,
gormandised the way the Dutch toss
pickled herrings down the hatch.

Enough rubbish you'd assume to choke
the drains of any gullet, until you catch
the rapturous return journey of song:
rococo notes that cry out for transcribing
on calf parchment with a calligraphy quill —
the opposite of magpies which, for all
their preening, can't rustle up a note

between them, scraping the barrels
of their rapid-fire throats;
pointedly attired in well-pressed
morning suits, though lacking in finesse,
rattling on about nothing,
jarring like a car struggling
to start, the ignition failing to engage.

But it's the thrush's tune
the light expires to, day slipping
through the gnarly fingers of old trees;
a music inducing the absurd spectacle
of a man (myself, say) looking to a bird,
of all things, in a digital epoch,
for entertainment, maybe even truth.

So Much Depends

The red barn. The Vermont farm
you fled from to the city
or vowed you'd retire to some day.

The barn at your grandparents'
in Kansas where you stowed away
one preteen summer, happy

to be left alone, at sea on the prairie,
hay spilling before cutter blades,
waves breaking on an inland shore.

A battened-down barn, holly-berry red
against the first dusting of snow.
Chevron-patterned wagon doors.

The grocery store forty miles off,
an upstate Amish village planted
among neat-drilled horse-tilled fields.

There will always be room
in the scheme of things for a red barn.
You may depend your life on it.

Inhale cured fodder, grain, manure.
Admit winter cattle to the stalls.
This is your clapboard cathedral:

pillars, nave, aisles, weather vane.
Wheat is separated from
chaff here, sheep from goats.

Come back, Grandma Moses, lead us
from the desert of downtown
to the promised land of the red barn.

Vigil

Life is too short to sleep through.
Stay up late, wait until the sea of traffic ebbs,
until noise has drained from the world
like blood from the cheeks of the full moon.
Everyone else around you has succumbed:
they lie like tranquillised pets on a vet's table;
they languish on hospital trolleys and friends' couches,
on iron beds in hostels for the homeless,
under feather duvets at tourist B & Bs.
The radio, devoid of listeners to confide in,
turns repetitious. You are your own voice-over.
You are alone in the bone-weary tower
of your bleary-eyed, blinking lighthouse,
watching the spillage of tide on the shingle inlet.
You are the single-minded one who hears
time shaking from the clock's fingertips
like drops, who watches its hands
chop years into diced seconds,
who knows that when the church bell
tolls at 2 or 3 it tolls unmistakably for you.
You are the sole hand on deck when
temperatures plummet and the hull
of an iceberg is jostling for prominence.
Your confidential number is the life-line
where the sedated long-distance voices
of despair hold out muzzily for an answer.
You are the emergency services' driver
ready to dive into action at the first
warning signs of birth or death.
You spot the crack in night's façade
even before the red-eyed businessman
on look-out from his transatlantic seat.
You are the only reliable witness to when
the light is separated from the darkness,
who has learned to see the dark in its true
colours, who has not squandered your life.

David Wheatley

Sleepwalking

I want to feel it again: what I felt
when I woke once standing in the kitchen
after walking downstairs in my sleep.
The school bags had all been lined up
and the lunches packed in clingfilm
by the fridge, gurgling to itself,
but this was hardly the kitchen
of the evening before, the unusual shape
in the corner that was a brush then
could hardly be the brush that we used
for sweeping the tiles, and the goldfish
rubbing its nose on the glass of its bowl,
were I to hazard a finger, could
hardly but have developed a taste
for flesh, or so I thought.
I moved with the new-found awkwardness
of a woken sleepwalker across the floor
and towards the stairs and the more familiar
strangeness of dreams, but looked back
once to see it again: the kitchen
like a charcoal drawing, the table
set for my absence, this new place
I had seen for the first time
stripping of meaning the place that I knew
without a word or a struggle, threatening
only that it might become habitable.

Spleen

after Baudelaire

I've more memories than if I were a thousand years old.

An enormous chest of drawers in whose stuffed hold
you found poems, law-suits, billets-doux, balance-sheets,
romances, locks of hair rolled up in receipts,
would hold less secrets than my sad brain.
It's a pyramid, an immense souterrain
sealing in more dead than a mass grave.
I'm a loathsome cemetery no moonbeams ever pave,
whose crawling worms — just like remorse — once released
will always choose the sweetest corpse on which to feast.
I'm an old boudoir that's been filled with faded roses,
sepia tableau a forgotten style composes
out of gloomy pastels and engravings, trailed
in perfume some unstoppered flask's exhaled.

There's nothing that can match these limping days for length,
when our boredom, ground down by the silent strength
of snowy years, dismal and incurious fruit,
learns to live in immortality's salute.
Henceforth, living matter, you are nothing more
than a granite rock encircled by vague terror
snoozing at the bottom of a Saharan mist;
an old sphinx world-forgotten and oblivion-kissed,
on no map, and whose foul humours sing for no one
now except the last rays of the dying sun.

Giacometti, c. 1952

It is the clamped jaw
and boxer's hands that catch the eye

in the photograph, the index finger
pointing towards the ground;

the taste for perfection on speaking terms
with the dripping basement studio

and endless scruffy shirts. The figures,
Genet wrote, were offerings

to the dead, and death was gravity:
the wire-supported hands dimpled

the air like mayflies' legs on water
in their tiny miracle of balance.

Up they grew like rope tricks, the legs
left unattached and matchbox

Easter Island heads, the standing figures
and the figures striding nowhere

that were always where they had to be,
and as if already there forever:

their huge feet and few square inches
of base that could be Archimedes'

one firm spot; there, in another
photograph, a roomful of them

and just the artist's head grinning
in a corner, wondering whether

the best thing mightn't be to destroy
the whole lot now or work all night.

At a Yüan Play

The Soul of Ch'ien-nü Leaves Her Body

Ch'ien-nü,
since she bade her betrothed, Wang Wên-Chü, farewell,
has had no peace,
and marks the emerald stalks
in the bamboo grove
to count the days until he returns to her.

No Chang girl
for three generations has been married to
a man not in
the Imperial service;
her love has travelled
ten thousand miles in search of an appointment.

Long before
his return — she fears from her dreams — he will have
broken their vows.
Now he writes to her mother
confirming those fears:
he's coming home, and bringing 'the young mistress'.

Faithlessness!
Picture for yourself then the girl's reaction
when, returning
from the capital, her love
brings with him on his arm,
his unfailing companion of three years —

Ch'ien-nü's
soul, her walking double (stolen away
from her body to be
with him all this time), come
to rejoin her, their
two loves twice as strong now in a single form.

A Garden in September

Inch by inch the oblong slab
of sunlight wins over the lawn;

we shift in the wooden bench hourly
to stay in the shade and watch

the cardinal purple of tangling hebe
and wide-open clematis embroider

the far wall, where ants scramble
and leaves cover snails spared

the attentions of midday.
I have only to spill a glass of water

for the sun to lap it up at my feet.
But summer is ending,

and for more than the worm
the blackbird twitches impatiently

before swallowing. The tarmac
that baked so long in the heat has burst

on a clump of underground mushrooms
already dead and beginning to stink,

and tomorrow something will be
not quite the same as we found it today

but still cause for neither regret nor alarm:
the chalked hopscotch grid in the lane

beginning to fade, the cat on the wall
picking its way more cautiously

through the scattered mosaic of jagged glass.

Autumn, the Nightwalk, the City, the River

How early the autumn seemed to have come that year,
the drizzles like moods, the tightness in the air.
Walking was different: nervous, brisker now
under the streetlights' tangerine conic glow;
needing gloves and scarves. I had both,
and a raincoat pulled up tight around my mouth.
Direction never mattered on those streets.
Once I walked all night and called it quits
somewhere miles from home, then caught the first
bus back. What mattered was being lost.
Anywhere would do: I remember suburbs
plush with hatchbacks parked on tidy kerbs,
privets, cherry blossoms, *nouveau riches'*
houses named for saints, complete with cable dishes;
and then the streets where every window was
an iron grid across its pane of glass,
the garden weeds in cracks, a noise ahead —
a bird, a cat — enough to make me cross the road.
Any light was harsh: all-night Spars
and the lit façades of Georgian squares
I'd hurry past; headlights glared like search-
beams in their hurtling, quizzical approach.
But landmarks were always a magnet. I'd be out
for hours — in sight of open fields — and spot
a pub or spire I knew, then find myself
being led by it, with inarticulate relief,
back in. Home was defeat but consolation too,
reassurance there was nowhere else to go.
The clubs all shut, town was deserted all over:
the only living thing would be the river,
and one night following it, I got a sense
of how, if anything did, it left the dead-ends
of the place behind as, sleek as a dream,
past barracks, churches, courts, the lot, it swam,
the lights that danced on its surface so many jack-

o'-lanterns promising no going back,
for it at least if not for me. I followed it
all the way to the quay-end steps and sat
as long as I thought it would take to reach the last buoy
and, dry land forgotten already, the open sea.

Visiting Hour

Puce, there is no other word
for the colour of the upstairs ward
I find you in behind a curtain,
the sheets around your chin and smarting
from the elegant needlework
you've been stitched up with, still too weak
to raise a drip-fed arm to hold
the flowers I've brought in from the cold.

Oxygen masks above their heads,
the women in the next two beds
are swapping family histories
like symptoms of a shared disease:
the son one hopes will settle down,
the daughter in London, getting on,
another who works too hard to take
the time to visit. Maybe next week . . .

Even for the dying time
to kill is at a premium
in a place like this, its leaden dance
conducted by the ward clock's hands
forever stuck an hour before meals —
even when dinner consists of pills —
or programmes hardly up to much
they'll wheel you from the ward to watch.

The contours of your supine frame
beneath the sheets alone can tame
my fears that, shock-haired, wild and grim —
a Cheshire cat without the grin —
your cradled head is all that's left
of the failing body that I loved
and placed in a stranger's hands to cure
of sickness at its very core.

Now excised. Taking your wrist
I feel your dogged pulse protest
its unconcern and stake its claim
to the slow reflux of health again
through startled limbs, however scarred,
whatever you may have endured
carrying on as blithely as
the hair on a corpse's head still grows.

Surprised or not to be alive
you find you cannot help but thrive
on daily gifts of grapes and roses,
life in homeopathic doses:
an upturned, half-read paperback,
birds in the trees, their weak attack
of song at dawn, your morning glass
of barley water the colour of pus.

Under it all the unspoken trust
you merit more than self-disgust:
the prospect of being able soon
to dress, wash, feed yourself alone –
regain, if not *élan vital*,
sufficient recklessness of will
to trade your place here for a bed
in the larger, roofless ward outside.

A loud goodbye from another room.
Your eyes have closed. I'm needed at home:
I let our fingers disentwine,
moisten your dry lips with mine
and stand uncertain how to leave,
embarrassed at myself, relieved
by a nurse's head around the door
calling time on visiting hour.

AM Radio

The static is
the sound of the world's
axis turning
as I finger the dial,

a chaos of voices
gasping for breath,
the short wave snoring
its dreams in white noise.

After-hours radio.
There is nothing to stay
awake for and nothing
to make me drift off.

Punctual, various
headlines leap time zones,
pips mark the hours
like morse ultimata;

one phone-in show host
keeps punting the dull
sludge of insomniac
chatter *ad nauseam*.

Sleep is beyond me:
each shake of my head —
half defiance,
half resignation —

stays creased in the pillow
I roll on. This smooth plastic
box devours sleep,
spits dreams out

and builds invisibly,
wide and high
as the room's four walls,
its babel in air.

And at odd moments,
unlooked-for, silence
descends between stations . . .
And it is as much

as my ear can do
to tell the radio's
tiny silence
from that of the night.

Misery Hill

Miserere, Domine . . .

Streetsign gone and most of the street,
high walls asterisked with wire,
impassable rubble victorious:
only the allure of a name
still on the map but nowhere else.

A name on a map but even at that
more solid than so many other ghosts
I have stalked in our snap-together capital
of forgetfulness — Blind Alley,
Smock Alley, Hangman's Lane,

Isolde's Tower. Names fade,
people forget. I pick through the debris:
a pram, a tyre, a handbag. The wind
rises, five o'clock comes: cars
drift down the quay past Misery Hill.

Grey of a low sky that is not
debauched white or compromised black,
but as if in essence one
with the rubble and the circling gulls,
an ideal colourlessness called grey.

Only the gods that are cranes can see
the wreckers' yard behind one wall,
the warehouse roofs, the funnels and steeples
holding the sky aloft beneath
the low banked clouds in which they dissolve.

The gulls' cry mixed with a churchbell,

the horn from a freighter moored on the quay,
fade; traffic fades. The river
nearby, ebbed to a trickle and stinking,
is soundless: cry out and no one will hear.

Here's a single high-heeled shoe
posed upright, still wearable,
and a poster for a concert last year.
Might its owner come back for the shoe?
Is there still time to buy tickets?

The wind lifts again, a post-office van
passes silently by with letters
for anywhere but this grim street
with its rubble and wire-topped walls,
featureless and empty besides.

FROM

Sonnets to James Clarence Mangan

Fishamble Street, the Civic Offices
turning the sky a bureaucratic grey
above a vacant lot's rent-free decay:
craters, glass, graffiti, vomit, faeces.
One last buttressed Georgian house holds out
precariously against the wreckers' ball
or simply lacks the energy to fall
and rise again as one more concrete blot.
Ghost harmonics of the first *Messiah*
echo round the Handel Hotel and mix
with bells long redeveloped out of use
at Saints Michael and John's, a ghostly choir
rising and falling until the daydream breaks . . .
Silence. Of you, Mangan, not a trace.

❖

While Dublin's 'mass of animated filth'
was being urged by Shelley to revolt,
a childhood slum, its beetles, damp and mould,
was loosening your flimsy grip on health.
An older brother mysteriously dead,
parents that you couldn't blame enough:
what better way to cast your home life off
than changing into someone else instead?
Of all the masks you donned, which one was you:
'An Idler', 'Peter Puff Secundus', 'M.E.',
'Selber', Shakespeare's 'Clarence', all or none?
Your self dispersed more than it ever grew,
a dizzy paper trail, your fate to be
a nation's anonym, 'The Nameless One'.

❖

Saved, scavenged for your mocking art
a few young loves more myth than fact, none
returned, make up your sum performance on
that 'perforated pump', the human heart.
Human loves, I mean: there was one other
hiding in your landscape of the lost,
disembodied as a famine ghost
but clinging, clinging to her poet lover
for dear death — that vamp Dark Rosaleen.
Gone in the teeth, her breasts dried up, with no
place but some ragged ballads to call home,
what desperate last chance could she have seen
in you to make her think your lines would sow
redemption in her cobwebbed, empty womb?

❖

A pain as vivid as it left you numb,
anaesthetised by drinking only to
awake again, called for a killer blow —
called for sixty drops of laudanum.
Which pain no sooner died than resurrected
and needed killing one more final time
(each time always the last), and you'd become
a vampire and its hunter, both addicted
to the same cheap thrills, the same cheap fix
that dealers on streetcorners still dispense
today like snow — a snow that turns to slush
in blackouts, bleeding gums and unsafe sex,
the search among the wreckage of your veins
for a spot to stick the needle in and push.

❖

. . . *Deliver us from evil.* I almost join
the tiny congregation — headscarved women,
a dog, some winos — in its terse *Amen,*
half hopeless affirmation and half groan.
The notices inside the porch remind
me of the prayer group and jumble sale,
the pilgrimage to Knock, and who to tell
about that pregnancy you didn't want . . .
James, for all your sinner's *grand guignol*
and tearful one-night stands with penitence,
your faith remained the same — in heresy,
the earthly kingdom of a 'ruined soul'.
I grace an empty poorbox with a tuppence:
Remembered in our prayers . . . Lord have mercy!

❖

A folio creaks open, coughs a decade
of stored-up dust into your praying face.
Wrinkled, foxed, strong evidence of fleas . . .
the book itself is scarcely less decayed.
The race is on. Your poems gather speed,
realising time is running out.
And not for you alone: leaking rot,
the barren harvests run to barren seed.
But at your College desk your books retain
their unavailing charm, a Provost's bust
still pledges learning's universal salve.
That can no more save the land from ruin
than spare you that incalculable waste.
That spectacle. Your country left to starve.

❖

The yawning earth absorbs another guest.
A knot of mourners plumed in heavy crêpe
thins to a single hooded, female shape.
Then no one. Corpse to bone to soil to dust,
dust to dust, then even that much gone.
I skulk among Glasnevin's plaster Christs,
the well-kept gravel paths and nettle wastes,
the rows of plots in search of . . . here's the one.
IHS: *In hoc signo*, 'I have
suffered'? They blend like the rain and sodden earth
as the sun drowns. A few late rays hang on
to probe the fading script. *In memory of* . . .
No farce of flesh and blood but, given birth
to into death, MANGAN graved in stone.

❖

Let the city sleep on undisturbed,
new hotels and apartment blocks replace
the Dublin that we brick by brick erase;
let your city die without a word
of pity, indignation, grief or blame,
the vampire crime lords fatten on its flesh
and planners zone the corpse for laundered cash,
but let your heedless cry remain the same:
'The only city that I called my own
sank with me into everlasting shade.
I was born the year that Emmet swung
and died my fever death in '49:
my words are a matchstick falling though the void
and scorch the centuries to come with song.'

Table Manners

The arguments starting earlier each time,
over coffee, dessert, the meal, the wine,

their evenings drifted into slow reverse:
trysts became appointments, chores and worse,

the nothing that they had to lose they lost
in selfish mental tots of what it cost

calling for the bill and tipping too much
rather than wait a moment more to catch

not even the last or second last bus home,
or rather, the separate homes they started from

and that had failed to lead to somewhere else;
the dinners abruptly stopping and the calls —

as simple, the realisation it couldn't work,
as crossing and uncrossing a knife and fork.

An Apple Pip

I'm tricycling in circles round the old orchard
when my grandmother calls me in from the front door.
Her lined hands, when she waves, are covered in flour.
There will be salad for dinner, cake afterwards,

then time doled out by a ceremonial ancient
clock in the living room with the tea and talk,
the smell of antimacassars and cigarette smoke
and the glass of barley water I never want

but still am given. Windfalls lie thick on the ground.
The trees are stooped by the weight of their neglect,
apples that no one has bothered to collect
again this year and that crumble to mush in the hand.

My grandmother is icing the dessert
as I meet my grandfather lumbering from the shed
to a chair at the fading tablecloth inside
and a muttered grace before the meal can start.

The kettle's smoking gun as it pours out a refill:
Sunday after Sunday every week
the same performance played out, so alike
each Sunday, so unchanging it could still

be going on and I still five years old
but for the moment when a future counted
on to stay like this gets lost, upended
into pastness and the memory of a child;

the bicycle careering into a nettle-
patch in the orchard, the burning and the stink
of liniment rubbed on where I've been stung,
and after that no going back to the saddle

unless to cycle backwards from now on,
out of the tangled roots and the nettle-trap,
back to the original apple pip
into which I gather all that's grown

and gone and give it all a second chance;
my long-dead grandparents restored to life,
a beetroot salad I pretend to like,
the windfalls falling upward to the branch.

Riptide

When the Hawk jet came down in the Humber, bedding
down with the dogfish and Roman remains,
you could point to your rush of foreboding
when it flew over, showing the strain

in the sub-concert pitch timbre of
its rip-roaring bark and ominous height
above our lately repointed roof
that would have passed briefly through its sights,

sights that would soon zero in on the river,
its sluggish affront to such predatory grace,
the foul-mouthed gulls well below radar
and the sudden allure of losing all trace

of its own radar trace in one last kill —
itself — in the parting tide for the Hawk
supreme in the air even now in its fall,
the pilot shot free like a champagne cork.

The Owl

after Baudelaire

Owl at my window, window owl,
under the sycamore's midnight eaves,
alien god whose red eye roves
while he sits tight and plays it cool.

No police 'copter or car alarm
can budge him from his airy perch,
unflappable, who must keep watch
until the hour of perfect calm.

Look and learn: don't just do
something, stand there. Stand still and be wise.
Be the owl who does as he pleases.

Drunk on every passing shadow
man will always pay the price
for having wanted to change places.

Ariadne

Nightcrossing the ferry-threaded sea,
the endless islands separating them,
he sends her, waveborne, a thin meniscus
of his spunk. By morning it will reach
and dry upon her unsuspecting shore.
He's always been a charmer, right enough,
casting his vows on water, on the deep,

low down as only he knows how to stoop,
checking in each night and kissing off.
But what she hears in bed is the minotaur,
its low grunts turned to laughter at her rage:
at how the real labyrinth was Naxos;
how she is a prisoner now as much as then;
how it, not she, is the one who got away.

A Stone Head

'The wretched man 'gan grinning horridlie' — Spenser

Here's one for Dr Spurzheim's
phrenological cabinet,
paleolithic department:

the coroner's chisel records
no purchase on this stone
head's flinty bump

of amativeness, waked
from its bottom-drawer guillotine
basket by the attendant

and placed before us, bowling
ball, cannonball good
for any target in sight,

the thin nose tracing a plumbline
behind the eyes, frank
as the handwritten dates where the neck

gives way, curling from sealed
lips a broad, devouring,
laughably absent grin.

Numerology

> *'The cartographer lists and draws fourteen bastions, fourteen wall-towers, fourteen main thoroughfares, fourteen monasteries, fourteen castles, fourteen laneways . . .'* — Joyce, 'The City of the Tribes'

Purity of heart is to will one thing.
A pair of Trinity squares, down for the week:
how could that salty longing not awake
by Galway bay, our hearts gone for a song?

Under the arch, over the Corrib, pent
in a guesthouse, working it out again, the six-
es and sevens of it, the algebra of sex,
the octopus arms and legs out for the count

come 'breakfast at nine', at ten... Waking to
elevenses, a sleepy one on one,
we get up to the angelus' round of applause,

the tilly of a kiss in the street: the two
of us in the city of fourteen tribes, awash
with fourteen shades of light that colour us one.

Macaw

Because the terrible hook-nosed scarlet macaw
will not leave me in peace I bring him tributes
of sliced fruit he scatters in raucous disdain,
whistle him tunes he knows far better than I,
begin sentences he interrupts me
to finish. Because he will as soon
have my eyes out as look at me through
the swivelling molluscs of his own two eyes
I cower and will myself small as the ripple
I make in his darting, aqueous humour
but in he dives after me into the black
pool of his stare and will not rest until
his maggot tongue has slimed the hand
he perches atop and he has trodden hand,
shoulder and head beneath his standstill march
and opened his wings over my head
to stand for a moment, the terrible wingspan
doing its clipped, furious worst as I cower
and cover my eyes in the black shadow
of every last scarlet, blue and green feather
and 'help!' try to shout, dummy to his ventriloquist,
'help!', and screeching he interrupts me
for the whole street to hear, 'Help help help!'

The Haunted Jigsaw

lines for a niece

Where is the pattern that hides in the jigsaw
shaken out across the floor?
There where it always has been, found,
and until then never been before,
in the haunted house with blackened windows
you tap on to summon the mournful face
of a ghost at the window looking in

from an outside far from yours and mine,
and fading harmless into his
as your touch fades and the dark comes down
and you remain in light to light on
the piece you need, the cornerstone,
that grants you alone the power to choose
which windows you open, which you close.

St John and the Eagle

Lindisfarne Gospels

In the beginning was something
or other — what was it? The saint's
parchment is blank, but from
the badger's snout will come the hair

for the brush, from the calf's
martyred back the vellum,
from Ireland the adze-headed scribes,
their insular majuscules, the DNA

coils of frets, trumpets and key steps
weaving a carpet of pages for you
over the sands at low tide:
from gall and indigo the green

and blue of your tunic, from heliotrope
the pinks and purples, and wrought
to its uttermost lapis lazuli
from Badakshan of the peaks

from which the eagle will swoop,
scattering doves as he goes.
Evangelist's bird, tired
of the easy kill, the flocculent hare

and deckchair legs of the deer
folding under a ton's worth of rapt
persuasion in its claw: from a thousand
yards up the eagle has spied

and will snatch from your hands
your book, leaving you only
a feather with which to scatter
and sow the Word in his

fugitive image, *imago aquilae:*
no sooner will you have finished
this page than talons will
puncture and carry it off.

Chemical Plant

'I am pure ohm'

Seventies   concept album cover:
green fields   round the chemical plant,
a torch   flared   in the breeze's shiver,
all the crop circles   you could want
and two smoke plumes   that go on forever.

Wind down your window   for a smell
of the muskily   igniting beast:
exoskeleton,   pure shell
of power   that hides   no pacing ghost
but only   purely living steel

slicing   through the riverside view.
Always there   but never seen,
let all humanity   be the few
hard-hatted shadows   that we join
to work   this chemistry we do

to feed the fire   firing the hum
that rises   snaking   from each tower
and drives   the chain reaction   home
that surges   when it finds us,   lover,
and runs to ground   through our pale flame.

The Teardrop Explodes

falco peregrinus

Why does the teardrop become a diamond?
Why does the diamond not hit the ground
at a hundred and eighty, two hundred and fifty
miles an hour, one wing in front
        and one behind?
The boy racer pulls up short
in the half-second before impact
and peppers the air with a shock of swallows
black as their fear.
The 'I' of his absent smoke trail plummets
like a thermometer off the scale,
        icing over
the zero of failure no
        rerun will assuage.
The god's-eye perspective has shrunk
        to a pinprick, escape
velocity slowed to the twitch
        of a nerve flaring
        his claws in rage.
The escaping swallows haul their way up
a glassy surface of tiny
        scratch after scratch.

Fintan and the Hawk of Achill

Am seabhac a néad i n-aill — 'I am hawk, my nest on a cliff'

Before the flood
was Fintan
born of a day
with the hawk
and surviving the flood
changed to a salmon
an eagle
a hawk
and a man again
possessed of all wisdom
knowing all magic
and the history of Ireland
born of a day
with the hawk who
the bitterest night
in memory
took shelter in
an eagle's nest
killed its young
told the mother
returning
of a colder night yet
told her
disbelieving
go ask the blackbird
its perch bent in two
it had stood there so long
who said
go ask the stag
whose antlers could fence
a whole field
who said
go ask the blind salmon
frozen tight

in its pond

one Bealtaine Eve

who said

if I am blind

it is the work

of the hawk who pecked out

my eyes one night

bitterer even

than this and is now

in your nest

nest the eagle

returning

found empty of

the hawk

who meeting Fintan

the pair began

to collogue:

fifteen years of years old   I am   five thousand five hundred years

put in the shape   of a salmon each spring
by the Bann the Suir   the Liffey the Shannon to suffer
stuck fast in the ice of Assaroe of the seals
came   the hawk
who plucked out   my eye

I took your eye   it was I took your eye

pulled out my eye pulled out my eye
recompense me my eye

I might peck out the other

five hundred years a blind salmon   fifty
an eagle a hundred a falcon   and now what I was
if I am anything
From each of your twelve   sons on the battlefield

I plucked hand foot or eye
bore off the hand of the Tuatha De Danann's High King
carrion bird to Cuchulainn himself feasting on
rivers of blood from the spears
of Naisi Conall Fergus Cuchulainn
whom wounded in battle I found
and perched on his face to peck out his eyes
felt his spear enter my flesh
its barb there yet I who had
borne off the bodies of champions and heroes
piglets and boars before Dáithí went east
too weary now to lift up a blackbird
who have flown here from the west
for your blessing O Fintan
that I may return there westward
my journey to die there tomorrow

O bird
I will travel
with you
we will fly
by the light
of my eye
you pecked out
and drink
from waters
that coursed
in the flood
we will die
on Achill
older together
than all
the world
and God and time
asking forgiveness
we will admit them
to the cold shelter
under your wings

The Treasures of a Folklore Beyond Compare

As a child I would perch in the tree-house and dream of scaling the tower on the mysterious German's land behind the estate. As a teenager my one desire was to play the pipes like Johnny Doran. Now my music has been and gone and my palms fall useless against my thighs.

The town of Rathnew is an unremarkable town, with its Wimpy bar and plaster Madonna, but here rests Doran, king of the travelling pipers, one chanter's toss from the Wicklow bus and its godawful radio station.

Among the most important effects on the pipes is the contrast between C natural and C sharp, as featured in so many piping tunes, Doran's version of 'Rakish Paddy' for one. Consider how differently he does it on his two recordings of that track, working the regulators each time like a pack of hounds on the chanter's trail.

At the time, forty years on, John Kelly, who duets with Doran on 'Tarbolton' and 'The Fermoy Lasses', still kept shop on Capel Street, and kept his fiddle under the counter. His fiddler's brow: sloped, confidingly, over the counter, through the window, as I walked by.

Some pipers play open, some closed. Doran played open. I prefer closed, but prefer Doran's open to any good reasons why I might prefer closed.

One thinks of Robert Johnson.

Hoist that chanter off the knee for those low Ds and Es, let the fox bark all it wants!

Pipeless today, I look up as the bus passes the cemetery and wonder where I have buried my music.

Sometimes he plays C natural, sometimes C sharp.

How I dreamed, as a child, of the tower on the mysterious German's land behind the estate.

Sinéad Morrissey

Among Communists

I remember smoke and faces that I knew
And the fact that I got in free; my mother
Taking money by the half-collapsed sink;
Posters proclaiming 'AN EVENING OF BRECHT'
And subtitled: *Bring Your Own Drink;*
Too much conviction to see through.

Europa Hotel

It's a hard truth to have to take in the face —
You wake up one morning with your windows
Round your ankles and your forehead billowing smoke;
Your view impaired for another fortnight
Of the green hills they shatter you for.

There was Fire in Vancouver

There was fire in Vancouver,
And we leaned out into the night to watch it
Set light to the East End.
It had taken stand on Commercial Avenue.

We marvelled at the darkness of the city,
All neon dulled by the superior flame,
And wondered would it bestow its dance
On the Ginseng Teahouse in Chinatown, on Jericho Pier.

There were no sirens, hoses, buckets even,
Scattering streets and 'Fire!' 'Fire!'
We seemed the only ones conscious of the bright crusade
And we watched with Moses standing in our heads.

Glaciers

There is no sea in my blood.
There is nothing that cannot be stopped.

God's wand is absolute.
Looking at glaciers

Jinxed into stillness —
I miss oceans in my head.

Awaiting Burial

Being born was as painful as this —
The crusade of the heart to bloom in mist,

The pull of blood
On everything the body had

To pump in a new direction,
The sliding dissection

Of water
And air —

Getting the heart to falter
And the lungs to breathe water

Requires
The tonweight of the sky,

A damaged hillside, night-time,
The tunnel you dreamt of, O

Sarah, speak to me, you've been through
The journey, was there light on the other side

To Look Out Once from High Windows

Cost you your railway lines, washing lines, sex on billboards
Seven feet high, pissing in gardens, smoking in bedsits, dust.
Cost you the choice you never made so you could be lost
In the closest way to being found: the quicksand of a wife, in-laws,
The decrease that children bring, or an attic full of yourself only
Only yourself and only as you tell it — wanking and lonely.

Underneath your choice lay the surest way of being found:
To pass all the marriages, births, and seaside hols by
On an express train through life that doesn't stop. It was the honesty
Of death you wanted. Its silence was stunning, like the white surround
Of an all-round prison wall. The way life broke down to enter it was what
You couldn't bear, making young girls' summer photographs so falsely
stopped

And irretrievable. To look out once from High Windows was to fly
Over the walls you saw in life, in life's renunciation
And beyond, and to accept that endlessness might mean resolution.
All words broke there. You stopped your various desolations colliding
By just looking up. You built your runway out of decimated love
And saw in flight how nothing could be left to lose or prove.

After the Hurricane

You saw the wind as the breath of God.
You couldn't help it. Your refusal of the ether
That would mist over death, got smashed to splinters
Like the Florida coastline, up-ended in rain.
There was too much rage in the sky for it not to be God's.

Perhaps it was your position under the window,
At the mercy of whatever startled missile
Made its appearance next —
A tree, a house, a woman —
Over your head. You saw a shower of cars

Spat out like sycamore seeds
And a landscape that trailed wires
In its rush to be pure.
You felt too temporary not to be answerable
To the power in the break up of hills.

My New Angels

God's old angels made us peaceful.
They had wings of love and explanation.
They brought us our destiny to lower our eyes
And let everything be for a reason.
There was no bewildering them.

My new angels are howling, hard,
And there are masses in heaven
For every snuffed out light on a back road.
Their rage is assured, ragged, unforgiving.
There is no perfecting them.

The Juggler

He must have practised for hours
Between the bins and the mattresses
Of a rented back yard
To dance the seven painted skittles
Off his fingers like that.
He has the game whittled

To art. God knows what
Anachronism he took up before,
Using medieval skills to stop
Time: he puts the clock back
Nine hundred years
With this side-show for a quack

Or diversion for a king.
Still, or because of the drain
Of things modern, we ring
Him with faces. He knows
How we anticipate failure
And that what he owes

His audience is a defiance
Of breakdown. We watch as his magic
Creates the radiance
Of a spinning blue arc, brought
Slowly to standstill. Natural begrudgers,
We are nevertheless caught

By the weightlessness, the controlled
Mechanics of air

With all the improbables cajoled
Into truth, we are not as far out
From faith as we were.

Monteverdi Vespers

for John McManus

The voices sing me to a dark room, with a wall
Three parts window and a grey sky. Outside
There's a terrace where gulls have stalled
On the eggbox chimney-pots. I hear them cry.

I know the knacks of gulls: after rain how
They stamp the lawns to fool the worms.
I know they fly to chimneys to be warm, cower
Nowhere, fought shell to be here, stern

As the shark and its off-shore wreckage,
Where I've heard they hover. *Jerusalem,*
The voices sing. City compacted in faith and damage,
The cry of gulls accompanies you with knowledge.

Sea Stones

It is exactly a year today since you slapped me in public.
I took it standing up. You claimed I just ignored it,
that I pretended to be hooked on the dumb-show of a sunset,
splashing, a mile off. Too hooked to register
the sting of your ring finger
as it caught on my mouth and brought my skin with it.

All the next day I rolled with a migraine
down a merciless gallery that was mercifully without sun.
Sloshed tea in the saucer when your name came up.
I couldn't stop the cup of my hurt
flowing over and over until I saw there was no end of it
and only an end to me. How promiscuous pain can be.

He gave me roses. The surprise of butterflies caged in the palms.
And sea stones with tracings of juvenile kisses, scented with risk.
I wrapped them in black at the back of a bottom drawer,
hidden in underwear. The truth — that you never were so vivid
or so huge as the second the street turned towards us
in shock — got dropped between us like a fallen match.

You turned away as the sun disappeared like a ship. And I,
suddenly wanting to be struck again, to keep the fire of your anger lit,
I bit my lip.

& Forgive Us Our Trespasses

Of which the first is love. The sad, unrepeatable fact
that the loves we shouldn't foster burrow faster and linger longer
than sanctioned kinds can. Loves that thrive on absence, on lack
of return, or worse, on harm, are unkillable, Father.
They do not die in us. And you know how we've tried.
Loves nursed, inexplicably, on thoughts of sex,
a return to touched places, a backwards glance, a sigh —
they come back like the tide. They are with us at the terminus
when cancer catches us. They have never been away.
Forgive us the people we love — their dragnet influence.
Those disallowed to us, those who frighten us, those who stay
on uninvited in our lives and every night revisit us.
Accept from us the inappropriate
by which our dreams and daily scenes stay separate.

Zero Visibility

That high up, stars hurt like showering flint.
We drove into Flagstaff shell-shocked and vulnerable.
All night the motel light flickered and buzzed,
as in the movie I'd already seen and scripted —
raw and flawless, shot through with falling stars.

The next day was opposite.
Our hands held at arm's length were stolen by fog —
trees, highways and hills were swallowed by distance
and then released again, tantalisingly, slow colour by slow colour.
Exposure was over and we held our breath for them.

By the time we touched the tipped lip of the canyon
there was nothing to see but breathlessness itself,
its urgent, insisting clouds. You said the earth
was veiling her enormous sex with vaporised tears
and bridal dexterity. If so, I preferred it that way.

I loved the white unrolling river
of her refusal as it stunned us on the banks,
stupid as hit fish, with our cameras and stares.

The Inheriting Meek

Your letter comes with the news that the lake blooms
earlier each year. As yet September is free of it,
but then as though *October* were carcinogenic,
and days could split degrees between them evenly,
the oncogene of the lake turns manic
as soon as the month names change. America storms, the world warms
and a soft algal stretch is beginning its reach
from the shadow of your cabin to the stone-stacked beach.
It shows the time-consuming ambition of the inheriting meek.

You say you lost millennial Christmas in a week
spent injecting the lake with oxygen,
and write a list of the wars you've fought with the dam
so far and lost, that were not as bad as this —
giardia, sabotage, evaporation,
the year of no rain when the lake drained to wrecks,
water skis, exhausted eels, a hub cap off your station wagon,
and Aucklanders brought their children
to stare at the reason for rationing.

This could mean a green, undrinkable eye in the face
of the forest, the irreversible failure of the water supply,
whilst the language of the luminous algae
is murmurous, like intestines, and quaintly victorious.
Stars miss themselves in the eye, but keep their trajectory.
How neat, you say, and mean it, abhorring stasis,
*all change is good. We are piling into a future
we will not escape from easily, if ever,
for we have eaten time.* The algae gather.

Stitches

There has been extravagance in speech
and every spilled, exploded word has been a stitch
in a blanket made for an imaginary baby.
The words went south where the sun was, but stayed hungry.

A name came in the third month. A face followed.
A hair type, a footprint, but the stitches showed.
Imagination's cloth too coarsely woven
for life to catch and cover stitching over.

And then blood. Inevitable, true.
Simple and strong enough to cut all falsehood through.
Later the screen said darkness — no spine, no heart.
And the stitches came apart.

Our Flower Garden

Consider the flowers in our flower garden, how they rot.
Such promising buds! Early and extravagant,
each an answer to the other's colour, each parting lip perfect.
Without warning then, bruised and upset, they let themselves drop.

Into nothingness, an abyss. We watched. Not storms, not frost —
we'd had none. The sun had loved them. Not drought —
we'd watered them. It was a bitterness rubbed them out.
Some wish spoken in moonlight. Some curse.

Such children as these disarm us with their refusal to impress.
How we coax and cry at their withered heads.
But they are resolute. Determined not to touch us
with their possibility, they choose death instead.

Across the hedge the neighbours' poppies soar.
We smile and wave. Behind their backs we roar.

Jo Gravis in His Metal Garden

Our Lady of Guadalupe appeared to a humble Indian Juan Diego,
and told him to build a church on the Tepayac Hill
but unless he could bring proof the Bishop would not believe Juan Diego
when Juan Diego told Our Lady of Guadalupe
she asked him to hold out his Tilma and there on a cold winter's day
she filled it with the roses of summer
then the Bishop believed Juan Diego and so a beautiful church
was built on Tepayac Hill
it is the most revered place of worship in Mexico
— from the wall of a church in Tucson, Arizona

From the window of the midnight-bound Vegas plane
Tucson flares in the desert — a cactus pricked by rain;
lit houses, lit highways and floodlit swimming pools —
a stunned bird in a basin, spreading its wings to cool.
The gaudiness of Winterhaven is visible from air
in the aftermath of Christmas. Down in the dazzle somewhere
Jo Gravis is sleeping in his metal garden. It took a year
of free time strung like stepping stones from hour to hour
to finally clear his yard of rocks and the herbs he grew
as a solitary failed commercial venture — ginseng and feverfew.
Each hour of work an island. As though delivering his heart
from alcohol, he struck down to the bedrock of a humble start
and stood there a long time, exposed and rarefied. At first,
he simply let the pictures come, withstood the thirst
and suffered the parade of soldiers, beggars, widows, orphans,
owls without trees and waterless swans and dolphins
until a gate latched in his mind and he had them forever.
He knew then he could commit them to metal to challenge
the weather
and started to build. Metal the medium and metal the message,
he turned trolleys into children, knives into rose petals
from the pockets of Juan Diego, miraculous, crimson,
a velvet gift of proof from a virgin in a vision
hardened against the sun. He peeled flesh back from the bone
and fooled no one. When his women with aerial hair were done

his kettle-headed men stood guard against them by a river
of headlights and bicycle wheels. Such honesty in silver
puts constancy in a peeled hand of wires against the sky
and hope in a speechless sort of prophecy —
a teddy bear bound with twine to an orange tree,
its eyes replaced with pearls. With all of these images
hard and permanent and real and safe in cages
Jo Gravis sensed a sweet deliverance, an end to motion,
and finally built himself a wooden bench to sleep on
surrounded by signs — their shadows on his skin a lullaby
to flesh in a fleshless gallery.

An Anatomy of Smell

It is the easiest part of the day — the ending of it,
here, with you, among sheets that smell of our skin.
I would know your skin in the dark: its smooth magnetic film
would bring me home and cease my being separate
with one blind touch. I know it again now, this expanse
of noise and light between us. It conquers distance.

Hallways of childhood friends had smells, family smells
that followed family members into school as stowaways
in coat sleeves and lunchboxes — slipped giveaways
of origin, of who made who, of what was left to tell
made suddenly clear in every detail as if recently rained on.
One was made of wine; one walked crushed by blankets
    even under sun;

one carried the antiseptic of insulin packets and coconut dust
about her, in her hair, and later what I knew by force
to be the thin, hard odour of divorce —
shipyard metal caving under sparks, spit, boot polish and rust.
And I knew also that whatever was in my hallway
was exposing the line and the set of my spine like an x-ray.

Now we too have an identity —
the smell of us is through our sheets and wrapped around
    our home —
invisible ink encoded onto bone.
We have wrought it as surely as any family
forges something wholly themselves and wholly different
and marks each child for life with the hidden nature of
    their generative act.

From you, the smell of the Tucson desert:
copper deposits, animal skulls, the chalk trajectory
of stars no cloud covers or stains, ochre and chilli.
From me, bog cotton, coal fires, wild garlic, river dirt.
And from the two of us, salt. When we move house
such genealogies as these will follow us.

On Waitakere Dam

for Charles Brown

You wanted to up-end the boat
and set it on the lake we lived by
because no one would know.
It was lavish with silverfish and looked
defeated, humped on its secret
like a hand. There was nowhere to go to

but the magnet of the middle lake
where a vapour sat wide as Australia —
as sovereign, as separate, as intimate
with daylight, as ignorant
of clocks and raincoats and boats.
It threw a soft, unwatchable shimmer

we would not be human in.
You dismantled a sky
as you tipped the boat over,
the nest of a possum was robbed.
The hull sewed outside-in
as you inverted the universe.

We bobbed in the reeds.
The trees lay down their crowns
beneath us, an underwater canvas
of spectacular women. Above us
the crowds of their branches were cold.
Black swans were nesting in the nesting place,

trees reared to the rim of vision —
we slid on to the centre. At night,
with no lights for miles, the lake
would glitter with the Southern Cross.
It smiled at us
with a million silver teeth.

We'd heard it roar with rain
and watched it coughing eels
over the dam's brim,
too water-sore to keep them any longer.
They fell flinching themselves
into s's or n's.

And now we sat stilled in a boat
in the centre, under the lake's shroud,
and the listening
was for the car of the caretaker —
weaving down from the Nihotipu Dam
with Handel or Bach on the radio.

Goldfish

The black fish under the bridge was so long I mistook it
for a goldfish in a Japanese garden the kind the philosophers
wanted about them so much gold underwater to tell them
    what waited
in another element like breathing water they wanted to go
to the place where closing eyes is to see

I understood the day I closed my eyes in Gifu City I saw Japan
for the first time saw what I had seen the gate to the Nangu
Shrine by the Shinkansen stood straddled before my head and I
held out my hands to touch it and felt changed air it wasn't
there but I walked into it continually and over the gardens full
of pumpkin seeds in the ground and wild red flowers over
    them they told me

they brought autumn and they were about my head also in
    Gifu City all pearled
in mist and happy as Japanese brides. I saw the JR crates
    on the night
trains that passed through stations and seemed endless and
    running
on purpose on time's heels on sheer will to cross Honshu
    one end
to the other money's own messenger fire down the line.
    And when you talked me through

Gifu one end to the other eyes closed I saw what I would never
have seen sighted a transvestite taxi driver set apart on the street
a lost person flowers by the pavement pavements for
    the blind I saw
music as pulled elastic bands drums as the footprints
    of exacting gods

I mistook the black fish for an oriental goldfish the flash
    of gold
on its belly meant it carried its message for the element
    below it
always one storey down Zen masters attaining one storey
    down and I,
falling into you, story by story, coming to rest in the place
    where closing eyes is to see

Night Drive in Four Metaphors

I want the woman driving I don't know never to stop
driving us by rice fields on the narrowest roads
that are straight as the line through the kanji for 'centre' —
The eye of an animal skewered and shown on its side.

The smoke from the factories lights up tonight as a gate to
    a fallen-down moon.
A moon on its back under the shadow of its circle is
    a unique moon.
It means home is under the weight of a stone and that brightness
    can come from under a shadow —
The whole weight of a cold ball breathing on it and
    look how it smiles.

The flats for Brazilian factory workers have shirts hung out
    on balconies to dry.
The shirts are coloured by game shows and adverts for shampoo.
Full as scarecrows, lines across and lines down of them —
The buildings are ships on a wind sea trying to sail.

And you beside me with your hair overgrown watching
    the other side of the world.
Imagine how the stars are split between my window and yours!
The join is unimaginable from under the roof of the car —
Two worlds split open to each other, stars spilling from each.

Between Here and There

No one seems sure of the reason why aprons
are tied to the necks of stone babies in temples.
The priest says 'honour'.
The guide to Kyoto City mentions 'cold
on their journey away from us to the heaven for children'.
I look at them squatting in Buddha-reflection,
wrapped up to the throat in teddy bears and trains.

❖

There's a graveyard for miscarriages under Ikeda Mountain
as stark as a bone field. No flowers, tangerines, sake or aprons
but a basin of stone bodies in two parts: square body, round head.
Like oriental soldiers contained by a wall, they would go walking —
spill over with all of the energy for life that fell out of them too soon.
Except that even in stone some bodies have opened —
loose balls in the basin where heads have rolled.

❖

Inside the biggest wooden building in the world
sits Japan's greatest Buddha. One hand raised as a stop sign to evil.
The other is flat, flat with comfort and promise, flat enough
for all of us to nuzzle his thumb. His lily flower opened.
His crossing was a falling into light.
Fall with me, he says, *and you'll be raised to the heights*
of the roof of the biggest wooden building in the world.

❖

When Nagasawa visits the house of the dead
he leaves at the door his camera and tripod
his champion karaoke voice his miracle foot massage
his classroom dynamics his rockhard atheism
and slips onto the tatami of the prayer room
as the man who can chant any you-name-it soul
between here and Ogaki to paradise.

To Imagine an Alphabet

Too far back to imagine
It all was dissolved
Under soft black strokes
Of a Chinese brush
Diminishing the fatness
Of original things

Animal legs and human legs are emptied of flesh and blood

Patterns from flattened
Ants or a lake drained the facts
That are trees in winter
The spokes of the world went down
In a language that
Went everywhere, stayed put

Put out what you want a woman and man to be the picture
    will hold that too

There are stories in skeletons
And after the three fluid
Lines that are Mountain, the four
That are Fire, Ice as a stroke
On the left side of Water —
Problem is Tree in a Box

I hear moaning and see constriction in a picture the colour
    is cinnamon the taste is chalk

A mind is inside the lines
All of it and sooner or later
Sex is everywhere, money
Rice fields wives are mostly
Under the roof to like
Is Woman with Child

I get lost in a landscape of noisy ideas that cross and flare in
fireworks of strokes

Like a child who paints a smile
Over signatures makes Yin
And Yang (two kissing fish)
A rising sun in a field
Of wheat I draw windows leaking
On the Kanji for Rain

I make my moon round my forest has branches my people are
walking with arms and a head

And then murder comes, a second
Killing, so softly I'm deaf
At the second of entrance.
My pictures defy the eyes.
I see Lamentation as five falling stars,
Grief abroad and walking,

And a terrible stag, flames shooting from his heart, as he prepares
to walk and preach.

The Wound Man

for Federico García Lorca

It would have been a kind of action replay,
only worse. The white handkerchiefs.
The unimaginable collapse. The day
the markets crashed and unleashed
unknowing through the New York streets

saw you transfixed, a witness in Times Square,
as the world went down in hysterical laughter
and diminishing shrieks. Then thudded over.
All hope in the gutter, blooded and lost. How you loathed
the reflections of clouds in the skyscrapers

and the glittering rings of the suicides.
It was all one in New York: the manacled roses, oil on the Hudson,
financial devastation. Had you survived,
Federico, say, Franco's henchmen,
or the war that was to open like a demon from his person,

or the later war, and all the intervening years
between that fall of faith and this, what would you think?
Would you know what has happened here,
the way we do not know what has happened? Where
would your fury go? We shiver on the brink

of an ending, and a war stretches in front of us,
we stand where you stood. As for me,
I see the Wound Man walking, tall and imperious,
through the streets of America, surly
and muscular, from the textbook of Paracelsus.

He's been badly hit. There are weapons through every part of him.
A knife in the cheek; an arrow in the thigh;
someone has severed his wrist bones, on a whim,
and thrust a sword into his eye.
They've flung razors at his flesh to pass the time.

And yet he rears. Sturdy and impossible. Strong.
Loose in the world. And out of proportion.

Polar

after Brecht

My darling, lest you vanish back
to the vast frontier you fled from
once its darkness
failed to break —
baying for bathwater, bedlinen, *me* —
without a further word,
allow these gifts:

six pairs of pearl-stitch knitted socks,
an Aran with a fingered ridge, a scarf
to trap a boulder in.
For even though you're lean
and craven, I'd rather have you
round and down and rollable.
I want to hap you up —

so that you stagger off, surrounded
by my warmth, on your journey
north. I want to wrap
your delectable backside
(which I chew on so immoderately
when I'm out of my right mind)
in all the wool of Scotland.

Forgive me this redress. Forgive
the need to staunch my loneliness
on your enormous absence.
Even the furniture sags without you.
I invent a war to send you
off to, but it's only a war
with nature. They say it's winter

when you're up there
nine months of the year
(the solstice dragging its feet
with the weight of the planet);
that the sky is merely on fire
with its own futility; and the snow geese —
inconsequential company.

Contrail

Nightly now, insomnia lays its thumb
upon my forehead — an any how, Ash Wednesday cross.
Which, instead of insisting *Thou Shalt Pass*

to the Angel of Anxiety, hovering over the stairway,
beckons it in, at 3am, to unsettle me gently
with its insidious wings

Sometimes my mother and father.
Sometimes neither.
Sometimes childlessness, stretching out into the ether

like a plane

Genetics

My father's in my fingers, but my mother's in my palms.
I lift them up and look at them with pleasure—
I know my parents made me by my hands.

They may have been repelled to separate lands,
to separate hemispheres, may sleep with other lovers,
but in me they touch where fingers link to palms.

With nothing left of their togetherness but friends
who quarry for their image by a river,
at least I know their marriage by my hands.

I shape a chapel where a steeple stands.
And when I turn it over,
my father's by my fingers, my mother's by my palms

demure before a priest reciting psalms.
My body is their marriage register.
I re-enact their wedding with my hands.

So take me with you, take up the skin's demands
for mirroring in bodies of the future.
I'll bequeath my fingers, if you bequeath your palms.
We know our parents make us by our hands.

Flight

There he saw one Anne Bridlestone *drove through the streets by an officer of the same corporation, holding a rope in his hand, the other end fastened to an engine called the branks, which is like a crown, being of iron with a great gag or tongue of iron; and that is the punishment which magistrates do inflict upon chiding and scolding women; and he hath often seen the like done to others.*

— *England's Grievance Discovered* (1655)

After the murder of our blessèd Martyr,
After the slaughter of the rout at Worcester,
His son the rightful king went into hiding —
Here as a woodcutter, there as a serving-man —
Disguising the telltale milk-white of His skin
By the dye of rotted walnuts. 1651:
The Year of Our Lord that my husband bridled me
And I have learned to hold my tongue in company.

❖

He could not remain unrecognised for long,
Majesty being so natural unto Him,
It soon shone forth. But was He loved!
He walked upon the bones of England,
Sought solace at farms and hid in the crowns of trees
And all of nature shadowed Him. His enemies
Sifted the land and still His face was not revealed.
It is my love of Him bleeds when I speak out loud.

❖

He has stood in a fall of rain
While Cromwell's men sang psalms against Him
And did not venture in. He has seen women
Sink to their knees and then raise their hand in blessing.
My husband desires a sign.
But for all his reading of *Revelation*
I say heaven admits its own
And it is Him. The jaw-straps tighten.

❖

The changeling Prince vanished to France.
Deadwinter dismembers us.
Christmas consumes its own bright fire
And blazes by its absence. There is too much law
To live by, and I have torn my face
In two by swallowing silence.
My husband leads me through the marketplace
As the village women gape.

Pilots

It was black as the slick-stunned coast of Kuwait
over Belfast Lough when the whales came up
(bar the eyelights of aeroplanes, angling in into the airport
out of the east, like Venus on a kitestring being reeled
to earth). All night they surfaced and swam
among the detritus of Sellafield and the panic
of godwits and redshanks.

By morning
we'd counted fifty (species *Globicephela Melaena*)
and Radio Ulster was construing a history. They'd left a sister
rotting on a Cornish beach, and then come here, to this dim
smoke-throated cistern, where the emptying tide leaves a scum
of musselshell and the smell of landfill and drains.
To mourn? Or to warn? Day drummed its thumbs
on their globular foreheads.

Neither due,
nor quarry, nor necessary, nor asked for, nor understood
upon arrival — what did we reckon to dress them in?
Nothing would fit. Not the man in oilskin working in the warehouse
of a whale, from the film of Sir Shackleton's blasted *Endeavour,*
as though a hill had opened onto fairytale measures
of blubber and baleen, and this was the money-
god's recompense;

not the huge Blue
seen from the sky, its own floating eco-system, furred
at the edges with surf; nor the unbridgeable flick
of its three-storey tail, bidding goodbye to this angular world
before barrelling under. We remembered a kind of singing,
or rather our take on it: some dismal chorus of want and wistfulness
resounding around the planet, alarmed and prophetic,
with all the foresight we lack —

though not one of us
heard it from where we stood on the beaches and car-parks
and cycle-tracks skirting the water. What had they come for?
From Carrickfergus to Helen's Bay, birdwatchers with binoculars
held sway while the city sat empty. The whales grew frenzied.
Children sighed when they dived, then clapped as they rose
again, Christ-like and shining, from the sea, though they could have been
dying out there

smack bang
in the middle of the ferries' trajectory, for all we knew.
Or attempting to die. These were Newfoundland whales,
radically adrift from their feeding grounds, but we took them
as a gift: as if our own lost magnificent ship
had re-entered the Lough, transformed and triumphant,
to visit us. As if those runaway fires on the spines of the hills
had been somehow extinguished...
For now,
they were here. And there was nothing whatsoever to be said.
New islands in the water between Eden and Holywood.

Stepfather

When Cathy came to New Zealand, my stepfather Charles
put on his woollen vest and Swan overcoat and peaked cap
with a rainbow embroidered on it and took us to see the waterfall.

He was a bushman: had grown up in the bush Up North
before ever there was a town the way Whangarei is a town today
with its flat whites and yellow taxicabs and Maori women drivers.
Yes,

had shouldered his way into adulthood, into being army-wed,
from the bed of an eel-breeding creek, on the back of a Kauri trunk,
against the hard flat palm of a forest that — decades afterwards —

had still not been felled. So he knew where to take us and how
to take us,
that winter afternoon, in the handclapping rain of the Waitakeres,
donning that pack of his as though he were back in Vietnam,

where all his booming dreams still happen, his casual jockey saunter
a bowsprit through the leaves, though he knew exactly what
we might find
and wasn't daunted. And yet how tenderly they would park their cars —

some even bothering to hood the steering wheel in chains —
in viewing spots anywhere along the Scenic Drive, before
    breaking off
into the trees, when he would get the call to go and find them.

He'd cut them down after days sometimes. The branches of Pongas
unfisted beside the railway line and the birds were indefatigable.
The rain was bringing the dark on early but you could still see

the entire steaming basin of greenery swallowing water
on your left side (my mother in her innocence asking,
the day she arrived from Ireland, *but who planted all this?*)

and Cathy and Joseph and Charles and I were increasingly more like
forked poles in a river than people as we came up to the mouth
of the train tunnel and waded inside. He could woo wood pigeons

just by talking to them and once one had rested on his hand.
Away from the thwack and clatter of the downpour and where
entrance and exit were two equidistant reminders of daylight

lived the glow-worms he spoke of, that were not worms at all
but a little boy's peel-and-stick galaxy, a lace of green needlepoint,
winking on after lights-out over the bunk bed. Out at the other end

and evening was gathering pace in the forest far faster than
    we'd predicted,
returning each towering layer of flax to one vast, dripping canopy.
By the rudiments of a siding shed — a rejected Korean asylum seeker

had survived here for a fortnight on trapped possums and
    stream water —
we angled ourselves for the climb and veered right, up through
    the breathing
trees, and what dusk there was had swung shut on a solitariness

of moss and lichen and spider orchids. Charles cut the way out
in front of us
without slowing, insisting we still had time, his mind — who knows —
on the nights he'd lain down on the floor of a Singapore jungle,

with only a net to shelter in, and the insects in the air had shrieked
so accusingly at every rigid angle of his body, he couldn't sleep.
It had been raining now for a week. The Waitakere Dam was full —

even from here we could hear it batter itself over the brim
and the waterfall was the same: choked and slick and incandescent
in the dim cave it had made for itself. Our breaths came hard

and alien in the clearing as we took its kiss on our skin.
Charles stood like a conquistador, hand on one hip, looking up.
But already I was imagining the journey back, down through
the slithering

dark, all three of us steady in his flashlight's wake, hitting
the railway track
and then on through the tunnel and then up to the steps by
the concrete expanse
of the dam face, and into the house near the watercress bank
where my life

had been riveted for months. Our homecoming chorus the hunger
of owls, fierce and unassuageable — *morpork! morpork!* —
and Charles cocking his head at the sound of them as though
they could speak.

Zero

for Joseph

Whatever else it was he stole from the East —
indigo, gold, a brace of abused and temporary women,
frankincense, the inevitable spice or two,
or the fruit that shed itself with such feral sweetness
on the tongue it begged re-naming —
Alexander also stowed nothing —
that double nick in the Babylonian plaque which,
of everything, was the easiest to store
(the women were a nightmare)
precisely because it lived nowhere
and therefore everywhere: in two spare horseshoes
angled together, in the kiss of a thumb and forefinger,
in the sigh at the bottom of a poured-out water jar,
in the memory of some noon-white city square
wherever luck ran out, or faith, or anger —
but
when Alexander delivered zero to the Greeks
they turned and saw (or thought they saw)
a wellhead blacken in front of them —
an incredulous, bricked-in 'O' —
unravelling into inkiness like a sleeve, the kind
you might toss a stone into and never hear the splash,
though you stand and wait, your ear awash in silence,
for an hour — and over it the bric-a-brac of kitchens appeared
suspended in the sunshine — knives, lemons, sieves, pots, bowls —
a funnel of dailyness, which the wellhead then swallowed
like a child, and, sensing where it could lead,
this number/no-number that would eat the world,
the Greeks turned back to Alexander in the advancing shade
and smiled: for there were still angles, there were still
three old angels skipping over heaven carrying harps and signs.

Caitríona O'Reilly

Fragment

This night-breathing deceives, it is so calm.
The headland glitters with beached faces, lunar stares,
a tidal moon-haul of wrecks and drownings.
Their gazes are blank and lasting,
outfacing constellations even, crystalline.

My mother feared the wash and plunge,
that huge pull from the loosening shore.
Night after night she surfaced there again
in the small hours, the shallows, panting:
her near death refreshed by nightmare.

A child, I shut my eyes like oysters
on the green light, weird particles migrating upwards
from the bed, from whose choked throat
arose the swallow-sound I'd closed my ears on.
Now as I watch her sleeping and submerged

I see them, those obsessive dead —
their watery features sea-blurred, merged, evasive.
I hold my breath above her sinking head,
dreading their opaque past and fossil histories,
inky and indistinct as night water.

Two Night Time Pieces

PISCES

Thirteen Februaries slept through
before I learned what going under meant.

Pale and thin as sheets,
the near fields burst free of mooring.

Then the turn of the tide,
the sea stack,

the pier-light's onyx eye.
Those teenage dreams

were cuttle-ink tattoos
describing blue-rinse mermen,

each muscular wave awash
with sex and phosphor.

I was awash and rocked,
rocked hard to wake

and woke, drenched to the roots,
my flannelette pyjamas stiff with sand.

SLEEP AND SPIDERS

It is too strange to kill.
The symmetry of its eyes,

its eight paired legs askew
on the lintel, exoskeletal

and tiger-striped, all digestion.
It looks sudden but is still

for hours, eyes on stalks,
awaiting news from hair-triggers

that might be legs or fingers
(the whole thing a claw)

come to touch me in sleep —
hammock from which

black shadows seep.
Stars go milky, then go out.

I wake at five to what five is —
a cold blue glow and a self

trussed, barely breathing,
paralytic with dreams.

They Do It With Mirrors

She could have sworn the door was double locked
or what was that inside keyhole for?

He left in the morning, turning his key
against burglars and junkies, while she

drooled on the pillow of their broken bed
dry-socketed, after a botched extraction.

The occupants of a hundred jigsawed homes
silted the city's arteries. He was another one.

She slowly rose. The dim, mirrored room
had cracked wainscoting, which let the wind

but not the light in. It was not their flat.
Over coffee, the locked door stared her down

till she could have snapped the key in its slot.
Never broken into, the toughened steel grille

on the window loomed as she recalled
the unreachable wail of a walled-up child

while smoke dribbled from a crack in the brick.
It was not their flat. Was nothing to be forced?

The windows opposite might well have caught
her white divided face as she proved herself just

narrow enough to step clear, as from her own bones.
He'd wonder where she was when he got home.

Sunday

The Liffey twists inside its stone confines,
heedless. It has long since abjured protest,

saving images of nothing
but the rains and whimsy of a city sky.

It gains a wider heaven at the bay perhaps,
but at its own expense.

We walk among the parts of a stopped world
in the meantime, hearing it go by.

The noise of tearing metal
in the quayside wrecker's yard has ceased,

just the one car, wind-rocked and upended,
groaning slowly. Its wheels still spin.

As though we'd stumbled on catastrophe
without a clue to where the iron giants went

that lived here once. They left
an architecture vacant-faced and angular,

with windows smashed or empty,
refusing reflection. Our contact seems

transgressive here, and our joined hands falter
nearing that squat god menacing skywards:

an abandoned crane, dangling its black clamp
like a pendulum halted over our heads.

Marmoreal

'Wonder ye then at the fiery hunt?'
— *Moby-Dick*

After this warmth the snow must come
to bleach our bodies clean.

It fills our mouths as it falls,
it muffles our cooling bones.

The years collect in drifts about us.
For every ink-stained tryst

there are a thousand blank pages.
And though they'll invoke us like doves

from the howling circle, we'll stare
in silence from our stone address.

Two eyeless statues under snow
blinded by their own bodies' whiteness.

Possession

That anxious way you have of closing doors
(like the brown of your eyes and hair)
was never really yours.
My arms and elongated nose were owned before —
fragments of jigsaw
in the rough art of assemblage whose end we are.

Sometimes I don't know where we live
or whose voice I still
hear and remember
inside my head at night. In darkness and in love
we are dismembered,
so that the fact of our coming to at all

becomes a morning miracle. Let's number
our fingers and toes again.
Do I love you piecemeal
when I see in your closing hand a valve-flower
like a sea-anemone,
or is it our future I remember, as the White Queen

remembered her pinpricked finger? All of you
that's to be known
resides in that small gesture.
And though our days consist of letting go —
since neither one can own
the other — what still deepens pulls us back together.

Cedar of Lebanon

The original metaphor
has become the last

that had a deltic beginning
that was fragrant
leaf-lipped and vermilion

casts its shadow momently
on the floor of the pit

Octopus

Mariners call them devil fish,
noting the eerie symmetry
of those nervy serpentine arms.
They resemble nothing so much
as a man's cowled head and shoulders.
Mostly they are sessile, and shy
as monsters, waiting in rock-clefts
or coral for a swimming meal.

They have long since abandoned their
skulls to the depths, and go naked
in this soft element, made of
a brain-sac and elephant eye.
The tenderness of their huge heads
makes them tremble at the shameful
intimacy of the killing
those ropes of sticky muscle do.

Females festoon their cavern roofs
with garlands of ripening eggs
and stay to tickle them and die.
Their reproductive holocaust
leaves them pallid and empty. Shoals
of shad and krill, like sheet lightning,
and the ravenous angelfish
consume their flesh before they die.

Anxiety

Something had made a killing.
A few small bones by the wall
were sticky with dark blood
but no parts of wing or skull

survived to tell me what it was.
What was it? By afternoon
the petrol-coloured rain had come
and washed it down the drain.

So I wondered if a bird
had ever been killed in a corner
by a wall, and moved off slow
like those pompous burghers

of Oslo do, in *Anxiety*.
But something had made a killing
and the corner worried me
with everything I had, not noticing,

killed. Like those sickish faces
underneath their stovepipe hats,
a yellow shriek of sky behind them
and beyond. It was like that.

Prayer

after Aleksandr Blok

Those who were born in the hollow years
are lost and wander blindly.
We are the offspring of Russia's terrors,
Her victims of helpless memory.

Years that left everything burnt and raw,
do you bring madness or hope?
The days of freedom and those of war
baptised us in a bloody stoup.

We are all dumbfounded: the siren
has stopped our mouths that cried.
Hearts that were enflamed now learn
to measure time in the void.

Let our final hours be shared
by the circling raven:
let those who are more worthy, Lord,
be with you today in heaven!

On a Dropped Feather

Until the feather tapers like an arrow
it's a stem of hollow smoky glass
unsnappable from root to subtle tip.
A grounded starling could survive the loss.
This ferny plumage where the shaft begins
is made of down too delicate for flight,
unlike the finny structure of the outer wing,
fashioned for soaring. Perhaps the taut
intrinsic music of a bird comes
from the staves on its small fledged limbs.
The feather's utmost fibres have all the colour
and congruence of shot silk. From the loud strife
and beating of wings in the sky somewhere
it fell like the notched blade of a knife.

Hide

Because it tells me most when it is most alone,
I hold myself at bay to watch the world
regain its level-headedness, as harbours do
when keels are lifted out of them in autumn.
This is not unconsciousness. Seen from above,
the trees are guanoed sea-stacks in a greeny cove
full of gulls' primeval shrieks and waves' extinctions.
Here birds safely crawl between the bushes,
wearing their wings like macs with fretted hems.
The air's a room they fill to bursting with their songs.
All day the common warblers wing it up

and down the scale, see-saw, hammer-and-tongs.
This is not aimlessness. It is something industrial.
A starling cocks its head at a blackbird's coppery top notes.
All I hear of them in the hide reminds me
that the body must displace itself for music,
as my body has, inside this six-inch slot of light.
What converges in a thrush's throat, burnished, tarnished?
Its news endures no longer than the day does.

Thinking of Simone Weil

By day it lives on the other side of the river
in the metallic light that shines through bridges,
light piercing its solitude. Later, its wing-rustle

is the sound night makes over brackish tidal water.
The crane watches, holding a granite pebble
in its featherless claw, as Giraldus tells it,

wakened by the fall of stone into water.
But if the stone escapes the bird's marbled eye
and its iron-digesting throat,

it can do nothing but roll on the floor of the river
to the mountainous blue of the sea-mouth.
Then the sea's concussive weight,

its vast disturbances of pressure, mill the stone
to quartz and its constituents: flint, chalcedony,
amethyst and agate; or again the parts of feldspar;

calcium, potassium, sodium, barium;
and light will flicker through the million minerals
speckling the waves on a deserted beach.

Augury

Magnetic winds from the sun pour in
and send our instruments akimbo.
Nothing runs like clockwork now.
As skeletal clouds unwreathe our exposure,
panicky citizens climb ladders to hammer
their roofs on harder. A crackle of static,
and the world's fat face is in shadow.
There are swallow nests under the eaves,
each with a staring cargo: six bronze bibs,
six black-masked, African birds. They dip
and snap the last bees up. A million M's
foregather with a million others on the sky.
This is the shape that memory takes.
For days they practise flying, then they fly.

Six Landscapes

I. THE RIVER

The coming night breathes an atmosphere
of childhood October in crisp light and wood-smoke,
and the guy ropes
sway in the harbour
while the black river pauses
between two tides,
shaping itself in shadow.

It is never changing, never the same —
the ancient trees of the rookery in silent commune
with the river's
different darkness
when we pass, and this time,
an egg-speckled kestrel
bullied by swallows.

A field that was mysteriously full of nothing
once but poisoned sparrows, a convulsive rain,
is brown earth now,
would not disturb
the bubble in a spirit level,
with a manhole like
a navel at its middle.

We wonder how will the river change, escape
development, or work its careless necromancy
on the next ones
to come here —
and who will watch its black dreams
shatter into figments
skulled and crossboned in light?

II. LITTORAL

By the campsite, travellers'
greyhounds lick the junk they find
and sniff along a wall sprayed

RELEASE IRA PRISONERS
and further on, HANG THEM ALL.
I pass a line of bollards

stuck with blue stones off the beach
like pins on a pin-cushion.
The theme is blue, or slate-grey

maybe, like the tame sea is —
its stones seem banded with blue
like pillows, mollified by

the sucked-in breath of the sea.
Its creamy exhalations
leave them quite unmoved, just bruised

darker by the toppling tide.
I stare, in a slate-grey mood,
pretending nothing's realer

than the colour of the beach-
stones' blueness. Which is less like
blue the further down you go.

I select seven of them,
seven stones totalling home:
a dark one scored with crazy

yellow strokes like fossil grass
or hopscotch on a pavement,
a flat one like a mountain-

ridge in outline, capped with snow,
one like a mesolithic
axe-head, but more beautiful,

smooth basalt flecked with sequins,
one crossed with mineral lines,
one rock ringed like a planet,

one riddled with reddish specks
the texture of crayon wax.
An ostrich-egg of granite.

III. UGGOOL

For Seán and Jessica Lysaght

It was only when the road ended
and the engine stopped ticking
that we noticed the silence
that was of space unfolding
and ourselves absorbed by it,
unburdened by the light's extension.

Seen from the hill, Clare Island
hung between identical elements,
neither air nor ocean, and a list
of islands ran to the curve of the world.
I recognised the feeling:
we brought the weight of us to leave

at the rim of a perfect water,
or our idea of it, not the peat stream
underneath the senile thorn tree,
but this strand with its kelp straps
and shell-scourings, that furnace-boom
along the country's vanquished edge.

IV. THE AVENUES

Any other year I would have watched
across the bay and seen the fold of a horizon,
the weather move south. Here, it catches
me asleep. The gleam of new snow

enters my room like the sound of a horn
on the fog-bound Humber. Strange that in a place
of so much sky there is just one view,
but it is England, and to each his own portion:

between the cracks on my neighbour's frozen pond
and the saffron throats in my crocus garden
there is no relation. Daily, the brownish stain
from the tannery chimney smudges the sky

to which the black bare trees are lungs.
I keep my side of the bargain, tamping
down the tulip bulbs, uprooting the weeds
in my walled half-acre, letting the cat in

as the kitchen windows glow at five o'clock
and human noises seep between the hedges.
Down the darkening cinder-path, fenced at both ends,
their children's voices cry to me like owls.

V. ON BEVERLEY COMMON

'Here is unfenced existence'
—Philip Larkin

The minster's gold stones
tell of a settled polity
the minstrels on the walls
sing and fiddle
fiddle and sing
to the yeomanry
their mouths agape
their music now reaching
those nearer stars
and at the town's edge
this draped landscape
pasture rising to meet
the sky and someone's
herd wandering where
Clare might have sat
and not wept at fences
elephant limbs of the elm
flowers whose names
we have forgotten
and the thorn tree's
mezzotint trunk
plates in a closed storybook
the chestnut drops a lime
spatulate leaf where
the silence waits
O presences
and in the green cathedral
birds pipe from the eaves

the fox's topaz eye
hesitates

VI. IN ARAGÓN

Caspe — a parched sigh
the earth emits at midday

when the sun's reign heightens
over hills of yellow or pale orange dirt,

studded with agave harsh enough
to have and keep its liquid core.

Seventy years since,
this earth quenched itself

to some forgotten end
(any arid cone could be another),

the Ebro holds itself still inside
its dark blue dream, and the trees

twist with the effort of rising.
In Caspe, light pours through the gap

the hills create in being at odds
with each other against the flaming sky,

and shows their horizontal faces
grooved and inscrutable in the Spanish way

and as indifferent to the force that shapes them,
giving them fractured hearts for their fractured bones.

Poliomyelitis

The pool at the centre of the broken-tiled room
was once a swimming pool for local boys

with boils on the neck and chilblained knees.
Their old joints murmur like the sea's

gradual encroachment on the choked-up
gorge of nineteen-fifties *noblesse oblige*:

grass sprouts from the rafters of the Big House
now, like hairs from a pensioner's nose.

The swimming pool was long ago condemned
though a rusty ladder still dissolves at one end

and even the gulls won't land on water
this brackish and rancid. I carry the taint of it

away like my father, bend over it in dreams
to watch the dead plants thrive beneath the water,

the pocked silt open and the nymphs rising
to invade another element, breaking the surface

till the room's air fills with black butterflies
brushing their wings against my mind's ceiling.

Lag

Although it is the hottest day of the heatwave, clouds
are hauling their sackcloth bellies over volcanoes,
leaving silvery animal
or mineral traces behind.

The liquid will never seep far enough down
to kill that angry flicker in the earth's throat.
Seams of live fire
like snakes or veins are feeling

the surface. The extinct naturalist with his primitive camera
could tell the whole story with his burnt bones,
only they do not speak.
And this is what I wake up in —

mornings where it rains and I have forgotten my name.
What lapses from an eye not quick enough to see
ivy hooking itself to a tree,
how the numb foliage explodes?

Gravitations

March: the grey atom
I've swallowed drops,
element-heavy plumb line

to this year's mood —
as mercury might smash
its instrument —

drops through vapours,
humours, that acrid
snarl of the gut that,

stretched, would circle
the house, the city,
the planet on which

my feet stood,
when last I looked.
I am six months

nearer the earth.
I have barely moved
all winter.

Faces pass
as though their owners
went on wheels.

And still it drops
stopless, niagaric —
is it the principle

of gravity in me —
that waking
is falling, lying still

is falling?

The Maze

I live in a space that was bequeathed me,
a ziggurat of stepped spires and corridors.
          There is no road out.
Mornings, solar rays puncture the spiral,
and the unsheathed cornea shrinks
          like a snail at an object —

the corners, the slanted ends on everything.
There is an itch, and sometimes,
          among the whorls
of the breast's adhesive coral, a filament of blood.
What rises at this is the sound of the maze,
          a red noise that pounds

through aortic roads and storm-drains
in which, like caves, I have tried to hide.
          Nights are the worst,
spent under the thin grey blanket, listening
to the shifting rumours issue through the routes of the maze,
          waiting for what rises.

There are no words in the maze, no signs
pointing a way through the puzzle that daily distends,
          infecting mountains and fields
and all the city's membranes. And like a city,
what was loved and entered, or ignored,
          dilapidates, an eyesore.

Inside these wincing walls, things are not
what they seem. I must be more watchful
          for what rises
within a lidless dark that never splits,
as I pass again through its twisted routes,
          mislaid perspectives.

I never remember the road,
though I take it nightly. Each night
          the light lessens.
Each night new pathways open to terminate
like shut valves or lopped thoracic branches,
          nowhere.

X-ray

A vertical chain of spine:
flesh cloaks the bones'
articulation in shadow.
The Tree of Life, but not
of Knowledge: shot through
with this god's radiance, light
shook from his metallic hair,
the gravity of his glance
decreeing me unscrolled
as the killer might decipher
his victim, delicately
parting the belly's vellum.
I am lain against the plate
and dazzled: the light inimical,
the weight that enters weightless.
A thrown shadow dissects
the self from what it was.
Can flesh become all shadow?
Not yet: as through a glass
brightly and fragile as a bird's
shine my long blue bones.

Floater

Just lying here in the angled
sunlight, watching the leaves
shadow-stipple my window,
it suddenly swims into sight
like a snaggle-toothed sea-beast

submerged until now,
jellied eel in my vitreous humour.
It could be a crayon-scrawl
high on the wall were it not
for those snake-tongue darts

and feints it makes as my eye flicks,
frantic to catch itself up.
What vandal took a house key
to the windscreen? I dangle it
in space like a puppet,

watching it creakily shift
its nodes and joints. Caduceus —
telluric snake on a stick,
casting off the dull cells
from its refractive coat —

littering the bottom of my eye
with its pile of minus signs,
its nest of hair, a worm-cast
or caddis-case from which
(invisibly) some brisk beast fled.

Duets

Underneath, her voice is
a whalebone-and-cambric
arrangement, a set of stiff stays

or pegs, well-hammered-in.
She is a house with firm foundations.
Her fabric pulls apart

in the upper floors only,
where something can be heard
fluttering with calculated frailty,

a coquette's attenuated eyelash
or lace-fringed can-can dress,
a spinning coin dropped

on a polished table,
an ornamental dove trapped
in an attic, beating tired wings.

Her voice has entered every corner of itself.
The boy's voice is an arrow pointing upwards.
Its flute-notes issue from an instrument

still half a sapling, with green feet in the ground
and a flicker of leaves around its crown.
It has the gothic hollowness

of cathedral pipes, a cylindrical sound,
which is the shape a boy's voice makes
crossing its own vast space.

Hierophant

It was the oldest, coldest place in England:
his face emerged as from a dark pool
that night, the indifferent calm eyes deep,
a reticence in the bridge of the nose, hands
white as cuttle-bones. As though I'd drunk
the winter sun from the fen, pale and cool
as the sea-shell curve of his lip, I sank
like a silver hoard beneath him in sleep.

Stalker

Eyeing my own nakedness in a broken mirror
as the red-coloured money changed hands,
I woke to a sound lighter than wind in dry grass
and listened again, marooned on the near side of sleep
with prickling palms. I turned on the light.
A spider on the wooden beam over my bed

resumed its wavering walk. I'd sensed the rasp
of legs like brittle fingernails in sleep,
that bunched torso hung from its knuckles,
so I hit it once and watched it drop,
legs curled in reflex to the shape of a net,
as if snaring itself in its own quick death.

A equals B. B equals C.

We are getting
from A to B.
We are getting from A

to B in our shellacked
capsule, accompanied
by this arterial hum,

this song of tedium.
Heat of grief—
the kind that tears

purport to cool
but never do —
hot as the place

from which they come,
and come. There is no
space left between

the broken white lines
for anything now
but outbreaks —

the fox's out-of-nature
stillness by the road,
our imagination of its

ruined eye, its famous
white snout. Also
these cousin-casualties —

hare dead in the dust,
holding the secrets
of its broken oval head.

We are getting from
A to B. Reflected trees
flow over the windscreen

and from the eyes inside
water tries to fall
like something natural.

A Quartet for the Falcon

I. THE MEWS

My falcon is snatched from the air.
It is the dark time. I have cast
sweet-smelling rushes on the floor
and the walls are unlimed.

I keep a lamp burning in here.
Outside, England dreams under
a mantle of legendary snow,
her trees stood bare, aghast,

her spine stiffened against winter.
History is yet to happen.
I have banished the tercel-gentle
beyond hearing, while my lady

waits her change.
I have hidden her creance and bells
sounding their chord of freedom;
her buttercup feet keep the perch.

Twenty nights I waked her, haggard,
till she flew to the lure and stooped in air
to dive into my flittered dreams,
fixing them with her stares and ways.

Now I have seeled her eyes again,
hiding their black beams
with a stitch to each golden underlid,
knotting the threads behind.

She cannot see the spider twitch
on the rafter, nor the lamp's slow flicker.
She is blind to her own change
as all men are but I, witnessing

The colours drop from her breast,
the mineral glint of her back
go shabby as the waned moon
under a tonneweight of shed feathers.

II. OPUS CONTRA NATURAM

I feed her decoction of diamond-skinned adder,
hawker's prophylaxis, proof against taint in the wing.
That she should absorb the snake's cunning
makes me her alchemist, rattling the atoms
in a vitreous well. Red sulphur, argent vive, even
1,1,1, trichloro-2, 2bis (parachlorophenyl) ethane:
solve et coagula. Behold the work of my hands —
dead metals litter the ground, my poor bird sickens
and will not rise until warmed by a flame to the limbeck.
I have made a sealed world to hatch heavenly birds,
Their flight a cloud-burst, a rain of mercurial feathers,
while outside the peregrine atom wanders
through field, seed and leaf, and through the egg's
chamber: thin-shelled and toxic on the eyrie's edge.

III. THE LURE

Snared in a mode of seeing,
the raptor's eyes unseel again.

Not an outline scarfing the blue wind
but several worlds unscrolling:

the chemical plant's logical conduits
glitter like the keys of a flute

while brown earth casts up
bones of its lost alluvial people —

shards of Delft in a Dutch landscape.
Abandoned churches ride the horizon

like high ships. She is caught in the rigging:
such details as flowers in dark grass,

calligraphic wings imped by a scribe
to fiat lux, or mantling their Marian prey.

Over a bleached Segovian plain the eye
seeks its eagle like the sky's pupil.

Aguila, describing a brutal circle.
Slow clouds tumble from the cooling stacks.

Anchor, tear-drop and cut diamond —
now her sentimental silhouette descends

to a swung horseshoe bound in leather.
It is the World, the Flesh, the Devil.

IV. THE CURÉE

The secretive hart turns at bay,
lowers his tines to the hounds' cry.
The sword enters the bull's heart —
                    still he stands,
          amazed on the red sand
as the stony unbeliever might,

who has seen God. Soon now
horns will sound *dedow*
for the unmaking. Beaters flush
                    the grey heron
          like a coney from its warren,
the peregrine's jet eyes flash.

They go ringing up the air,
each in its separate spiral stair
to the indigo rim of the skies,
                    then descend
          swift as a murderer's hand
with a knife. Death's gesture liquefies

in bringing the priestly heron down.
Her prize, the marrow from a wing-bone
in which she delights, her spurred
                    fleur-de-lys tongue
          stained *gold-vermilion* —
little angel in her hangman's hood.

Pollen

Lying with one eye open I can see
a yellow spot staining the clean sheet

I put there yesterday,
a fleck of yolk suspended

in albumen, gold coin at the end
of a barren viscous sea

for those brave enough to stain
their lives to gild the Virgin's mantle.

Their blood mixed with foam
dries to crackling on the shores of Spain.

Azafrán — the colour of evening sun,
the flavour of honey that never reaches

the lips, edging instead a labyrinthine Gospel,
spilling its light inside the borders.

Even now I can barely contemplate
its brightness in the eye of the bee,

how it dusts his muscular back
and grain for grain matches his gold

in the gasp of the calyx,
in the petal's ragged breath.

Biographical Notes

HARRY CLIFTON was born in Dublin in 1952. He received his secondary education at Blackrock College in Dublin, and earned a B.A. in English Literature and Philosophy from University College, Dublin (1974), where he later obtained an M.A. in Philosophy (1975). After teaching English language and literature at the Government Teachers College in Keffi, Nigeria (1976–1978), he then returned to Ireland and taught English and French at Blackrock College (1979–1980). Clifton moved away from education and worked in the Irish Civil service (1980–1988), including a period working at refugee aid programs in Thailand (1980–1982), before finally returning to teaching English language and literature at The New School, Assisi, Italy (1989–1991); English and media studies at St. Charles Sixth Form College, London (1992–1993); lecturing on Irish literature at University of Bremen in Germany (1994); and acting as Writer-in-Residence at the University of Bordeaux in France (1996). He has also held posts as Writer-in-Residence in the Department of Anglo-Irish Literature and Drama at University College, Dublin during the 1990s, and at Trinity College, Dublin (2003–2004). He spent a year in the Abruzzi region of Italy, which he documented in *On the Spine of Italy* (London: Pan, 1999).

He is married to the fiction writer Deirdre Madden. They lived in Paris for many years, returning in the fall of 2004 to live in Dublin. Clifton's first poetry collections and short stories appeared in 'New Irish Writing' (*Irish Press*), and *The Irish Times*. He had reviews and feature articles on travel published in Thailand, the Unites States, and elsewhere. Among his published poetry, there is *Null Beauty* (Greyabbey: Honest Ulsterman, 1975); *The Walls of Carthage* (Oldcastle, Co. Meath: Gallery Press, 1977); *Comparative Lives* (Gallery Press, 1982); *Office of the Salt Merchant* (Gallery Press, 1979); *The Liberal Cage* (Gallery Press, 1988); *At the Grave of Silone* (Honest Ulsterman, 1993); *The Desert Route: Selected Poems 1973–88* (Gallery Press/New Castle upon Tyne: Bloodaxe, 1992); *Night Train through the Brenner* (Gallery Press, 1993). He has also published *Berkeley's Telephone and Other Fictions* (Dublin: Lilliput Press, 2000).

DENNIS O'DRISCOLL was born in Thurles, County Tipperary in 1954. He has published seven books of poetry: *Kist* (Dublin: Dolmen Press, 1982), *Hidden Extras* (London: Anvil Press/Dublin: Dedalus Press,

1987), *Long Story Short* (Anvil Press/Dedalus Press, 1993), *Quality Time* (Anvil Press, 1997), *Weather Permitting* (Anvil Press, 1999), *Exemplary Damages* (Anvil Press, 2002), and *New and Selected Poems* (Anvil Press, 2004). The volume *Weather Permitting* was a Recommendation of the Poetry Book Society in the United Kingdom in 1999 and was also shortlisted for the *Irish Times* Poetry Prize in 2001; *New and Selected Poems* obtained a Poetry Book Society Special Commendation in 2004.

Dennis O'Driscoll is also a widely published critic; the critically acclaimed and influential book *Troubled Thoughts, Majestic Dreams* (Gallery Press, 2001) contains a selection of his essays and reviews. Among the American publications in which his poems have appeared are *The Southern Review, Yale Review, Verse, New England Review, Columbia, TriQuarterly, Poetry* (Chicago), *Poetry International, The Paris Review*, and *Harvard Review*. A civil servant since the age of sixteen, O'Driscoll works in the head office of the Irish Customs House in Dublin, Ireland. In 1999, he received a Lannan Literary Award as a "writer of distinctive literary merit" who has made "significant contributions to English-language literature." The American Academy of Arts and Letters selected O'Driscoll for the 2005 E. M. Forster Award. He lives in County Kildare with his wife, the poet Julie O'Callaghan.

DAVID WHEATLEY was born in 1970, grew up in County Wicklow, just south of Dublin, studied English and French at Trinity College, Dublin, and piano at the Royal Irish Academy of Music. While at Trinity he was an editor of the student magazines *Icarus* and *College Green* — an apprenticeship which has served him in good stead, for he is one of the founding editors of the journal *Metre*, 1996, coming out of England, Ireland and the Czech Republic. He completed his Ph.D. at Trinity College on the poetry of Samuel Beckett, a writer who has remained a primary interest and influence. Wheatley's first volume *Thirst* was published by Gallery Press in 1997. His second is entitled *Misery Hill* (Gallery, 2000), and a poetry-pamphlet entitled *Three-Legged Dog*, co-written with Caitríona O'Reilly, was published by Wild Honey Press in 2003. His third volume of poetry, *Terrestrial Variations*, is forthcoming from Gallery.

Wheatley has taught at several major universities in Ireland, and presently lectures at the University of Hull in England. He has won various awards (for example, the Rooney Prize for Irish Literature in 1998) and edited various anthologies, including *Stream and Gliding Sun: A Wicklow Anthology* (Wicklow: Wicklow Co. Council, 1998), and *I am the Crocus*, an anthology of children's poetry (Wicklow Co. Council, 1998). He is also an indefatigable literary journalist, with his literary reviews, articles and poetry appearing in *The Irish Times*, *The Guardian*, *Times Literary Supplement, and London Review of Books*, among other journals in the UK and Ireland, and in *The Southern Review*, *Raritan*, *Poetry* in the United States. His poetry has been included in anthologies, such as *The New Irish Poets*, edited by Selina Guinness (Bloodaxe, 2004). He recently edited a selection of James Clarence Mangan's poetry (Gallery, 2003) and is presently writing a book on contemporary British poetry from 1945 to 1999 for Cambridge University Press.

SINÉAD MORRISSEY was born in County Armagh in 1972, but grew up in Belfast. For her undergraduate work at Trinity College, Dublin, she studied English and German between 1990 and 1995, taking a year out of her studies to teach in Flensburg, Germany in 1994. After her B.A., she lived in Japan, where she taught English, and moved on to New Zealand, where she lived on the shores of the Waitakere Dam for a further year. She returned to Ireland in 1999. She was the youngest winner of the Patrick Kavanagh Award in 1990, but waited six years before publishing *There was Fire in Vancouver* (Manchester: Carcanet, 1996). She received an Eric Gregory Award from the London Society of Authors in 1996 for part of the manuscript of her first book. Her second collection, *Between Here and There*, was published by Carcanet in 2002. It received the MacCauley Fellowship from the Irish Arts Council, the Rupert and Eithne Strong Award (Ireland), and was shortlisted for the T.S. Eliot Prize in 2002. In the same year, she was the Writer-in-Residence at the bi-annual Poetry International Festival in the Royal Festival Hall, London, while, in 2003, she was one of four writers selected for the British Council Writers' Train project (six thousand miles by train across China in twenty-one days). In 2004 she earned a Ph.D. from Trinity College, Dublin for a thesis on the figure of the servant in eighteenth-century fiction. She is currently Writer-in-Residence at the Seamus Heaney Centre for Poetry, The Queen's University, Belfast. She has been anthologized in *The*

Field Day Anthology of Irish Writing: Irish Women's Writing and Traditions (Cork, 2002) and *The New Irish Poets*, edited by Selina Guinness (Bloodaxe, 2004). Her next collection, *The State of the Prisons*, will be published by Carcanet in April 2005.

CAITRÍONA O'REILLY was born in Dublin in 1973, grew up in Wicklow, and studied English and Archaeology at Trinity College, Dublin. She edited the well known student magazine *College Green* at Trinity and there also wrote her Ph.D. on American poetry (specifically on Emily Dickinson, H.D., and Sylvia Plath). She has taught in Trinity College, Dublin and St. Patrick's College, Dublin and has reviewed for *The Irish Times*, *Poetry Review*, and *Times Literary Supplement* among others. She is on the editorial board of the journal *Metre*, for which she has written numerous reviews and essays.

Her first collection, *The Nowhere Birds*, was published by Bloodaxe in 2001, and was awarded the Rooney Prize for Irish Literature. She was commissioned by the BBC to produce a radio poem, which was broadcast in 2003, and was awarded a Harper-Woods studentship by St. John's College, Cambridge, for travel to Spain in the spring and summer of 2003. Her academic articles include an entry on Sylvia Plath for the *Encyclopaedia of American Literature* (Oxford University Press). She has been included in various anthologies, such as *Staying Alive: Real Poems for Unreal Times*, edited by Neil Astley (Bloodaxe, 2002) and *Breaking the Skin: Twenty-First Century Irish Writing*, edited by Nigel McLoughlin, Matthew Fluharty and Frank Sewell (Ballyclare: Black Mountain Press, 2002), *The Field Day Anthology of Irish Writing: Irish Women's Writing and Traditions* (Cork, 2002) and *The New Irish Poets*, edited by Selina Guinness, (Bloodaxe, 2004). She is currently Writer-in-Residence at the Dun Laoghaire Institute of Art and Design.

PERMISSIONS

The editors gratefully acknowledge the permission of these writers and publishers to reprint the material in this book:

Harry Clifton

Poems from *The Liberal Cage*, *The Desert Route: Selected Poems 1973–1988* and *Night Train Through the Brenner* are reprinted with the permission of The Gallery Press. "Reductio," "Bare Arm," "Reading Saint Augustine," and "The Daughters of Lot"are reprinted with the permission of the Author.

Dennis O'Driscoll

Poems from *Kist*, *Hidden Extras*, *Long Story Short*, *Quality Time*, *Weather Permitting*, *Exemplary Damages*, and *New and Selected Poems* are reprinted with the permission of Anvil Press.

David Wheatley

Poems from *Thirst*, *Misery Hill*, and *Terrestrial Variations* are reprinted with the permission of The Gallery Press. "The Treasures of a Folklore Beyond Compare" is reprinted with the permission of the Author.

Sinéad Morrissey

Poems from *There Was Fire in Vancouver* and *Between Here and There* are reprinted with the permission of Carcanet Press. "The Wound Man," "Polar," "Contrail," "Genetics," "Flight," "Pilots," "Stepfather," and "Zero" are reprinted with the permission of the Author.

Caitríona O'Reilly

Poems from *The Nowhere Birds* are reprinted with the permission of Bloodaxe Books. "Six Landscapes," "Poliomyelitis," "Lag," "Gravitations," "The Maze," "X-ray," "Floater," "Duets," "Hierophant," "Stalker," "A equals B. B equals C." are reprinted with the permission of the Author.